EMYL JENKINS'
Southern Christmas

EMYL JENKINS'

Southern Christmas

FOREWORD BY CHARLES KURALT

PHOTOGRAPHS BY CHIP HENDERSON

CROWN TRADE PAPERBACKS ❧ NEW YORK

Design by Ken Sansone

ᕳ

"Love the Giver" (pages 89–90) is reprinted
with permission of *Victoria* magazine

Published by Crown Trade Paperbacks, 201 East 50th Street, New York,
New York 10022. Member of the Crown Publishing Group.

Random House, Inc. New York, Toronto, London, Sydney, Auckland

Originally published in hardcover by Crown Publishers, Inc., 1992.
First paperback edition printed in 1995.

CROWN TRADE PAPERBACKS and colophon are trademarks of Crown Publishers, Inc.
Manufactured in Singapore

Library of Congress Cataloging-in-Publication Data
Jenkins, Emyl. [Southern Christmas]
Emyl Jenkins' Southern Christmas / foreword by Charles Kuralt; photographs by Chip Henderson.
Includes index. 1. Christmas–Southern States–History.
2. Christmas decorations–Collectors and collecting–Southern States.
3. Antiques–Southern States. 4. Southern States–Social life and customs. I. Title.
GT4986.S6J46 1992 92-3411 CIP
394.2'68282'0975—dc20
ISBN 0-517-88479-8

10 9 8 7 6 5 4 3 2 1
First Paperback Edition

*F*or all who delight

in the joy and mirth of Christmas,

especially Susan Urstadt,

a Merry Southern Christmas

And in memory

of Aunt Mary

Contents

Foreword

BY CHARLES KURALT

I can see the cold moon shining through the branches of the sycamore tree and

casting shadows on the upstairs bedroom wall. I can see a little boy, five years

old, lying perfectly still under a pile of quilts on the featherbed. He is studying

the shadows and listening for reindeer hooves. I can feel his heart pounding.

It is my own heart. Back then, it was pure, and it beat in the chest of a true

believer. I knew the rules: "You better watch out, you better not cry, you better

not pout…" I had not cried or pouted for a month. And now the night was here!

This very night Santa Claus was flying through the air bringing presents to good boys and girls and bundles of switches to naughty ones. I lay in the silent darkness, breathless with excitement.

How good did a child have to be, or how naughty? Emphatically, I did not want a bundle of switches. I wanted a bicycle. My mother and father had told me a bicycle was too much to ask for, but I had written my own letter to Santa enclosing a picture of the bicycle I had clipped from the Sears, Roebuck catalog, and I had given the letter to my grandmother to mail. If he did not think I was old enough for a bicycle this year, I told Santa Claus, maybe he could bring it next year. I wanted to put the idea into his head. And now I lay still, listening for the landing of the sled on the roof, listening, listening…

The year was 1939, one of those Depression years when Santa Claus didn't have enough presents to go around. The place was the farm of John and Rena Bishop, my grandparents, a long way down a dirt road in Onslow County, North Carolina. The house had no electricity or indoor plumbing, but it had a warm kitchen where my grandmother baked sugar cookies in the wood stove in the days before Christmas. It had a formal front room, used only for weddings and funerals and Christmases, and there we hung tinsel and popcorn garlands on a cedar tree my father had found passed over by the loggers on the logging road. At sundown on Christmas Eve, my grandfather went out to the old bell that was mounted on a post in the side yard and gave it a good ringing—an invitation to anyone passing by on the road to come to the house for supper. (No one ever came, but the old man continued that custom until he died, because he remembered his own father ringing the bell on Christmas Eve. "In those days," he said, "sometimes someone would come, and we could feed him, and never even ask him his name." I live in a city now, and feel bad for having no bell to ring.)

And after supper, by the light of a kerosene lamp we made a pot of hot chocolate, not forgetting to leave a cup on the hearth for Santa Claus, and a plate of cookies for his reindeer. We hung a big wool hunting sock for Santa to fill if he chose. And I climbed the stairs to the spare bedroom, undressed in the dark, wriggled between the cold sheets, and began my rapt vigil with the sycamore shadows. "He knows when you are sleeping, he knows when you're awake…" But how could he know for sure? I would be very still when the sled landed on the roof and close my eyes tightly. I tried it. I closed my eyes.

I woke in the light of morning. I ran down the stairs in my pajamas, into the front room, and straight to the hearth. The hot chocolate cup was empty! The cookie plate held only crumbs! He had been there! I looked up at the sock. It was lumpy and full. I could see a bright orange and a striped candy cane poking from the top. He had been there! He had come down the chimney and filled my stocking and drunk our hot chocolate right down!

I was so dumbstruck with joy that I didn't look farther than the hearth until my mother and father had come into the room, pulling on their bathrobes.

"Why, look here!" my father said. I looked. On the other side of the Christmas tree, propped up on its kickstand, was a bicycle, bright red, with a silver bell mounted on shiny handlebars.

I walked over to that bicycle, afraid to touch it. I felt a thrill like no other of my life, before or after. I thought the bicycle might be meant for some other little boy. I thought Santa might have left it in his haste by mistake.

"Nope," my father said. "Seems to be your size. I think it's yours."

Later in the morning, Buck came by. He was a little older than I was, the youngest child of the black tenant family that lived a mile down the road. He wanted to show me the new belt he got for Christmas. I showed him my bicycle. He said, "I'll teach you how to ride it."

I spent most of the rest of the day watching Buck ride around and around on the dirt of the side yard, bumping over the sycamore roots, circling the black pot my grandmother used to wash clothes, speeding down the hill to the corncrib and barn, and peddling back up again, jingling the bell. "You see," he said, "it's easy!"

I was glad when Buck's sister finally showed up to fetch him home. Since his riding lessons hadn't helped me a bit, I ran beside the bicycle for a while, pretending I was riding. Before dark, I found a rag and wiped the dust from the fenders and the spokes of the wheels, and when the bike was shiny and new again, I parked it back in the front room to keep it from getting cold at night.

This is a prideful and materialistic story, I know. But I excuse myself; I was only five. And anyhow, there *were* spiritual elements to that Christmas. There was the sacrifice two loving parents made to give their child a present they barely could afford; the closeness of family—the baking of cookies together and the decoration of the tree; and the virtue of sharing: I think I kept myself from hollering to Buck to give me back my bicycle.

I have warm memories of many Southern Christmases, of candles in the windows, of country ham and sweet potatoes on the table, of carols on the Victrola, and of a homemade holly wreath always on the door. Christmas is the best of Southern seasons, but the best Christmas was the one when I was five, before worldliness and wisdom began to set in. That year, great gifts came flying through the air, free for the wishing. I wish every child one Christmas just like that.

All it takes is faith. Weeks later, playing in the attic, I came upon a big cardboard box and made out the printed words on the side: "Elgin Bicycle. Sears, Roebuck & Company." This did not shake my belief at all. I raced downstairs to tell everybody the news: "Santa Claus left a box for the bicycle in the attic—for when we have to move!"

Old customs! O! I love the sound,
However simple they may be;
Whate'er with time hath sanction found,
Is welcome, and is dear to me.
                    Old English poem

Why Southern Christmases?

Last Christmas, a delicate yellow jasmine vine put forth a few golden trumpet-shaped blossoms as if to herald in the season. Woven among the silky throats, ribbons of dark-veined, hunter-green ivy lay undisturbed—until a single robin, content to fly no farther south than North Carolina, scratched the sun-kissed earth, pecking at berries fallen from the holly tree above. Ah...a Southern Christmas with birds and flowers, holly and ivy, and sunshine.

Sometime in mid-December, Southern magnolia leaves turn from a shimmering summer green to a deep, waxy winter green. Cascading over white

15

Even wealthy plantation families shared rooms during the festive Christmas season when dances, food, and company beckoned. In the Readbourne Stair Hall, built circa 1733 in Centreville, Maryland, now at Winterthur Museum in neighboring Delaware, the Queen Anne walnut daybed might have slept two young children.

or fanfare, a clear nippy December day invisibly replaces the lingering balmy Southern breezes of just the day before.

In Southern homes from Kentucky to Texas, families scurry about in preparation for the holidays. The time has come to gather pine and boxwood. Heirloom silver must be polished. Mile-high stacks of Grandmother's best china—oyster plates and butter pats included—are taken down from high pantry shelves. On the sideboard fashioned from plantation-grown deeply grained walnut, the brasses never gleamed brighter. Only the best is fine enough for this most special of all holiday celebrations.

Why Southern Christmases? Just what makes Southern Christmases so special? Is it their festiveness? Or the South's acclaimed hospitality? What accounts for their unmistakable charm? Though other sections of the country also have their own, equally unique and endearing styles, what is the irresistible appeal of Southern Christmases both past and present? The answer lies mostly, I believe, in rich traditions rooted in the history and heritage of the South—and, interestingly, the answer also lies, at least partly, in the North.

You see, I know both North and South well. In fact, I have had the best of both worlds. My father, from whom I inherited my respect for industry and hard work, is from New England. And I have a Southern mother who gave me my love for laughter and sentiment. Early on I learned the differ-

fences that line the streets of Aiken, South Carolina, heavy boughs of holly fruit change from burnt-orange clusters to thick masses of deep, Christmas-red berries. Far away, on the same sun-kissed day in a long-abandoned rock garden in Huntsville, Alabama, a fragile periwinkle blossom warmed in the tangled vines opens out of season.

Later that night, though a ring around the moon above the mountains of West Georgia portends a dusting of snow, the only white covering nature sends is a blanket of silvery stars against a cobalt blue sky. The very next morning, quietly, and without fail

ence, a difference that came down through the centuries.

Historically, there are two indisputable reasons why Christmas has been so special in the South, even during colonial times. The first has to do with human nature; the second, with Mother Nature.

If your image of an old-fashioned New England Christmas is one of jingling sleigh bells, festive spirits, and toasts of good cheer exchanged before a blazing fire, Oliver Wendell Holmes's lamenting recollection written at the end of the nineteenth century may shatter some of your illusions: "The Boston of my youth [the early 1800s] was still half-Puritan Boston, with the 'unutterable ennui' of its Sundays....It was a Boston with no statues, few pictures, little music outside the churches, and no Christmas," he despaired.

Another venerable New Englander— even her name reflects her Puritan ancestry—Hezekiah Butterworth—began her 1880s' tale "My Grandmother's Grandmother's Christmas Candle" this way: "There were no Christmas celebrations in my old Puritan home in Swansea, such as we have in all New England homes to-day. No church bells rung out in the darkening December air; there were no children's carols learned in Sunday-schools; no presents, and not even a sprig of box, ivy, or pine in any window."

But in the South! "The great fête of the people was Christmas," wrote Thomas Nelson Page in 1892. "All times and seasons paled and dimmed before the festive joys of Christmas. It had been handed down for generations....It had come over with their forefathers. It had a peculiar significance. It was a title. Religion had given it its benediction. It was the time to 'Shout the glad tidings.' It was The Holidays....Christmas was distinctively 'The Holidays.' "

In the plantation South, which was quite different from the industrial North, Page tells us, "Time was measured by it; it was either so long 'since Christmas,' or so long 'before Christmas'....The corn was got in; the hogs were killed; the lard 'tried'; sausage-meat made; mince-meat prepared; the turkeys fattened, with 'the old big gobbler' specially devoted to the 'Christmas dinner'; the servants' new shoes and winter clothes stored away ready for distribution and the plantation began to be ready to prepare for Christmas."

Today, thank goodness, there is little difference between a Southern and a Yankee Christmas. Across the country we celebrate a twentieth-century American Christmas filled with joy, laughter, great cheer, warm spirit— all blended and stirred together. But these days we have television and travel, and families brought together through marriages that unite many different cultures, countries, religions, even races.

This was not so during the seventeenth and eighteenth centuries, when regional differences reflected a unified philosophy and a

In the colonial South, Christmas was a season, not just a day, of festive celebrations.

A wooden rosary, a
time-faded icon, and
a small bowl of holy
water provided a
makeshift altar for
Spanish soldiers far
from their Catholic
cathedrals at Christ-
mas in sixteenth- and
early seventeenth-
century Florida.
On the table, cheese,
bread, and oranges
brought to Florida by
the Spanish explorers,
are covered by
protective netting.
The Oldest House, a
National Historic
Landmark, owned
and operated by the
Saint Augustine
Historical Society,
Saint Augustine,
Florida.

homogeneous culture. Take the North, for example. From our school days we remember that the first settlers who came to Massachusetts, Rhode Island, Maine, and New Hampshire were seeking religious freedom. But their motivation was much more deep-seated.

These Puritans came to America not just to have the freedom of their own beliefs, but to escape the influences of the Anglican and Catholic religions. Any ceremonies that resembled Papist or Episcopacy doctrines, even Christmas, threatened the core of their beliefs. So on Christmas Day, 1620, the Pilgrims left the *Mayflower* and went ashore, not to give prayers of thanks, but to begin "to erect the first house for common use to receive them and their goods." There was no Christmas celebration that day on which "no man rested" in Massachusetts. What a contrast to the "Merrie Ole England" tradition of the Yule log and carols!

Things were no better on December 25 of the following year. Governor Bradford found a group of freshly arrived "lusty yonge men" would not heed his instructions to stop playing in the street, "some pitching ye barr, and some at stoole-ball and shuch like sports." So the stern governor "tooke away their implements, and tould them that was against his conscience that they should play and others worke. If they made ye keeping of it matter of devotion, let them kepe their houses, but ther should be no gameing or revelling in ye streets. Since which time

nothing hath been atempted that way, at least openly."

During the ensuing years, penalties were inflicted for such joyful activities as dancing, wrestling, ringing bells, and dancing around the maypole—that most joyful Elizabethan English tradition—until, in 1659, the General Court of Massachusetts passed a statute declaring that "anybody who is found observing, by abstinence from labor, feasting, or any other way, any such day as Christmas Day, shall pay for every such offense five shillings."

And so, Christmas passed quietly, solemnly, for years, even centuries, in Puritan New England. Around the mid-nineteenth century, as the Puritan religious fervor softened and news of Queen Victoria's joyful Christmas celebration with her family spread to America through *Harper's Weekly* and *Peterson's Magazine*, New England Christmases became festive occasions.

But it might also be that the Union soldiers, returning north from the Civil War, took some of the spirit of the Southern Christmas home with them. Though I haven't seen that suggestion so boldly put forth in any books, one report in 1861, the first year of the Civil War, did mention that the Yankees in a Richmond, Virginia, military prison were "in a high state of enjoyment, singing, laughing and shouting, as if their present position was improvement upon anything they had been accustomed to at home."

Another Southern account, this one an

Games and whimsy were forbidden in seventeenth-century Puritan New England, but in the South, "merrie thoughts" would come throughout the year to the one who got the "big end" of the Christmas turkey wishbone. Adam Thoroughgood House, Virginia Beach, Virginia

impassioned 1862 editorial, reminded the Northerners, "Christmas has ever been a day of peculiar festivity and enjoyment in the south, which has inherited the reverence of it from our Cavalier ancestry. It is a day which has brought joy to the mansion and the

Stories of past Christmases are forever endearing. Liberty Hall, Kenansville, North Carolina ∾

cottage, the master and the servant, and has never been dimmed by a cloud till the present unholy war!" After seeing my Southern mother's unspoken influence on my New England father over the years, and reading the accounts of Christmas in the South during the Civil War, I wouldn't be at all surprised if the North didn't take a great deal of its "new" Christmas spirit from the South.

In contrast to the joyless, self-deprecating Puritans of New England, the seventeenth-century Southern settlers were adventurers seeking wealth and commercial success in the colonies. Unlike the Puritans, they were not running away from religious persecution. They traveled to America with

hope and high spirits. They were cavaliers in the fullest sense of the word.

The Virginia colonists were devout members of the Church of England, and kept the spirit of the Christmas celebration from the start. One hundred settlers had started out for the New World. Seven months after they arrived in Jamestown in May, on December 25, 1607, the surviving forty colonists gathered before a wooden altar to give thanks.

How vividly we can see them in our mind's eye now, for Captain John Smith left this description of an early, makeshift "church" in the Virginia wilderness: "Wee did hang an awning, which is an old saile, to three or foure trees to shadow us from the Sunne; our walls were railes of wood; our seats unhewed trees till we cut plankes; our Pulpit a bar of wood nailed to two neighbouring trees. In foul weather we shifted into an old rotten tent...."

And the joyful account of the Virginians' second Christmas is in vivid contrast to the stern story of Governor Bradford's Christmas Day edict in Plymouth Rock the year after the Pilgrims' arrival. At Christmas in Jamestown in 1608 the Indians and colonists, now at peace after Pocahontas's rescue of John Smith, feasted together on "plentie of good oysters, fish, flesh, wild foule and good bread."

Jamestown and Plymouth Rock. How often we think of these as America's first Christmases. But there were other, earlier Southern Christmas celebrations.

*In Charleston,
South Carolina,
handwoven baskets,
popcorn-and-holly-
berry wreaths, even
freshly picked garden-
grown paperwhite
narcissus line the
streets at Christmas
time(above). I bought
the basket for Chip and
Cindy Henderson,
the wreath to add a
tangible touch of
Christmas to our
travels, and the
bouquet for my own
pleasure. Then Wil-
liam, Sarah, and
I got down to serious
shopping (left).*

Few people are aware that America's very first Christmases were celebrated in Florida, near Tallahassee. In 1539, Hernando de Soto and his 600-member expedition were led in Solemn High Mass by three of the thirteen priests who had accompanied them to the New World. But soon after de Soto's death in 1542, the conquistadores returned to Europe. A more permanent colony was established in 1565, when another group of more zealous Spaniards founded a garrison town of St. Augustine to protect their Florida colony while they searched for new riches. It was there that the true, first continuous celebration of Christmas in America began—its roots in Catholicism, not Protestantism, as most people believe. And so America's first Christmases can be traced to sixteenth-century Catholic services in Florida and seventeenth-century Protestant services in Virginia. In both places, Christmas was a day of religious thankfulness when time was taken to pause, to celebrate the meaning of that most special holy day.

Popcorn berry and creeping cedar wreaths sold in the downtown market area of Charleston are a timeless South Carolina Christmas tradition.
∾

Yet another reason why Southern Christmases laid the foundation for today's American Christmas is the weather. The relatively mild (when compared to New England's) winters brought the naturally warm, hospitable Southerners together.

"Pretty cousins came for the festivities," Thomas Nelson Page exclaimed. Sally Skipwith Kennon bragged that she had had a most delightful Christmas at a house party because she and her girl friends "had all the beaus in the county with us."

"We had forty guests who remained all night, and the following day and night, so you may know I was busy to make them all comfortable [in] such cold weather. I had nineteen or twenty beds, and thus stored them away, two by two," wrote Miss Livy Battle from Cool Spring, North Carolina, to her sister in 1855.

"In the course of redeeming my Pauns, I had several Kisses of the Ladies!" wrote Philip Vickers Fithian from Virginia on December 23, 1773. "Early in the Evening came Colonel Philip Lee, in a travelling Chariot from Williamsburg. Half after eight we were rung in to Supper. The room looked luminous and splendid; four very large candles burning on the table where we supp'd, three others in different parts of the Room; a gay, sociable Assembly, and four well instructed waiters!"

Pretty girls, throngs of sociable friends, backgammon, card and parlor games. Southern friendships and hospitality are so

legendary that those many years ago Fithian, who incidentally was a Princeton-educated "plantation tutor" in Virginia, suggested that the Southern air imbued "all the Inhabitants with Hospitality."

If such were the case, the Southern air Fithian was referring to was filled with December's nippy breezes, not warm June zephyrs, for in the South the winter—not summer—months brought the farmers out of the fields, into their homes.

At the same time, the cold weather packed down the Southern dirt roads that were often either dusty or muddy in the spring, summer, and fall months. Snow,

sleet, and ice come in the South most often in February and March. Christmas, with its good traveling conditions, leisure time, and festive atmosphere, became the traditional season for gatherings. The excuse, if one were needed for this extravagance, was friendship.

Neighbors traveled to see one another. Country relatives journeyed to the city, and city relatives visited the country. Either way, they stayed, not just for a day or two, but sometimes for weeks, busy with parties, dances, music, courting, weddings, and in ensuing years, anniversaries. From isolated Virginia plantations to the cobblestone streets of bustling New Orleans, to the highlander

Summer evenings held little leisure time for plantation owners with crops to tend and harvest, but long, dark winter nights were passed playing games and discussing politics. De Mesa-Sanchez House, St. Augustine, Florida
∾

towns in the Shenandoah Valley, when Southerners came together at Christmas their days were filled with festive times, quiet times, and nostalgic times.

Imagine a jovial New Orleans Papa Noël in the midst of a taciturn Boston family or the frivolous shooting of muskets on Christmas Eve in staid Providence! Such festivities simply couldn't have occurred in stodgy eighteenth-century New England.

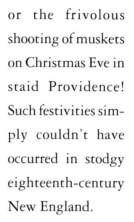

Throughout the South, heirloom silver and grandmother's best china are used each Christmas for dinner.

Southerners have such a natural affinity for Christmas, it should come as little surprise to you that the first states to declare Christmas a holiday were Louisiana and Arkansas in 1831, and Alabama in 1836. The New England state of Connecticut followed in 1843, seven years later. Massachusetts didn't "legalize" Christmas until 1856, but then it must have come with great joy. On December 24, 1856, the Boston *Daily Bee* wrote, "Christmas, it should be bourne in mind, is now a *legal* holiday."

Though the people of the South seem to share a common convivial bonding, the geography of the region is wonderfully varied. In Maryland a shivery December morning may begin when the yellow-red sun brings a clear, bright day across the small state. In Louisiana or Texas that same sun may rise an hour later, coming up behind a smokey fog that will hide its light till mid-morning. Then the full-blown sun will turn the sweater-weather morning into a shirt-sleeve afternoon.

From farm scenes in Virginia and Alabama of barnyards home to sunning cows and calves—to the automobile-filled streets of Atlanta, Washington, and Houston, every corner of the South has as many distinct personalities as it has inhabitants.

Through the centuries, some of our Southern Christmas traditions have come from faraway parts of the world while others have grown anew. Whatever their source, wherever they are currently found, traditions in the South are deeply cherished and soon take on their very own "Southernness."

Yes, memories of a long-ago South are as close as the front doors of the stately homes and humble cottages that have withstood the crowding-in of the twentieth century. And new traditions are budding every year.

Thank goodness today you don't have to be Southern "born and bred" to enjoy the felicitous spirit of Southern Christmases. From Tennessee to New Mexico, the South is home to all who delight in laughter and little pleasures, to anyone with a benevolent heart, and particularly to those who cherish glimpses of the past and find joy in the present.

So to touch the spirit, to enjoy the variety of Southern Christmases firsthand, one November day my photographer, Chip Henderson, his wife, Cindy, and their three children, Nicholas, Sarah, and William, aged almost-one through five, and I—Southerners all—climbed into a van and started out on our grand adventure.

On our journey, as we approached strangers, soon to be new friends, how often I recalled Robert Beverly's words written almost 300 years ago as he traveled through Virginia: "The Inhabitants are very Courteous to Travellers, who need no other Recommendation, but the being Human Creatures. A Stranger has no more to do, but to inquire upon the Road, where any Gentleman, or good House-keeper Lives, and there he may depend upon being received with Hospitality." In fact, should a visitor come to a house with "but one Bed," Beverly assured his readers that the host would "very often sit up, or lie upon a Form or Couch all Night, to make room for a weary Traveller, to repose himself after his Journey."

Of course no one ever had to give up a bed for us, weary travelers though we were at times. But each door was opened, and led to more doors being opened, as we were greeted, welcomed, and made to feel at home from Norfolk, Virginia, to Natchez, Mississippi.

Still, during our six-and-a-half weeks on the road we could gather only a fraction of the rich Christmas celebrations and traditions that live in the South. Even with planes and interstates and 65-mile-an-hour speed limits, we couldn't possibly visit every nook and cranny—each with its own endearing tales that weave the fabric of Southern Christmases through the ages.

But we did find the joy, the spirit, the beauty, the love, the *fun*, and the indisputable charm of a Southern Christmas everywhere we went.

And we, like Southerners for generations, made memories of that very special Christmas spent traveling throughout the South that will last a lifetime. May these pages add joy to your memories of your own Southern Christmases. For it is memories that keep alive a glow in our hearts that is as warm as the embers that glow in our hearths at Christmastime.

The lights of the John Wright Stanly House provide a welcoming glow to a dark December night in New Bern, North Carolina.

Christmas D*ecorations*

"WITH IVY DRESSED"

Never am I happier to be in the South than on those days when the time comes to gather Christmas greenery. I really don't know why it is called greenery though, when there are so many other lovely Christmas colors in the South.

There are hearty orange pyracantha berries, iridescent green Christmas roses, peppermint red and white camellia blossoms, lime-green smilax clusters, blush-pink star magnolias, translucent mistletoe, spikes of jet-black liriope seeds, sun-kissed golden pomegranates, paper-white narcissus, sprays of yellow jasmine on deep green leafless stems, lavender rosemary, cherry-red

Chinese holly (above), quince blossoms (right), and camellias (below).
❧

holly berries, prickly brown pinecones, boughs of hazy-green bayberries, shimmery yellow-tipped spires of mahonia, and my favorite of all, small, teal-blue cedar berries.

Many years ago, a Northern friend of mine asked if I'd please send her a box of ivy, mistletoe, holly (lots of red-berried holly, I remember), and pine boughs (with as many cones as possible). "Yes," I replied, "if you'll send me just a little bit of snow." "You can have Christmas without snow," she said, "but Christmas wouldn't be Christmas without holly."

How true, I mused, remembering lines my mother half spoke, half sang, every Christmas: "Be merry all, be merry all, with holly dress the festive hall." I haven't any idea if the lines are from a song or a poem, but I do know that even today we can't have Christmas until we've decked the halls with boughs of holly.

There are many reasons why those hours spent cutting and clipping December foliage are so pleasurable in the South—not the least of which is the excuse to be outside. I once read that during New England winters everyone looks forward to spring. We in the South have springlike winter days that make us want the winter to linger longer.

For in the South winter trees and shrubs have a beauty unlike that at any other time of the year. But they must be seen on a bright, crystal-clear day, of which there are many. On shady, overcast days, everything looks the same. On blue-skied days, when the sun streams through the thick covering of dark evergreen leaves—turning the deep brown tree limbs into a golden honey-brown—and rests upon fresh ruby-red berries, nature's colors brighten your heart and lighten your step.

Scooter, our amber cat who wears the color of fall year-round, always goes along on my adventure. Invigorated by the crisp air and the warm Southern sun, he steps high, despite his advancing age. Next to the regal holly by our front door there is a maple tree whose spreading branches grow low, close to the ground. While I reach as high into the holly as I possibly can to cut boughs that won't be missed, Scooter bounds across the leaf-strewn lawn and shinnies up the maple tree, proudly venturing out onto the tree limb closest to me.

Later in the day he will find his own nest of earth-warmed leaves, a spot on the northwest side of the house where an ivy-covered brick wall shelters him from any

cool breezes, and he will sun himself. (I once remarked to the children that I've never seen a cat sun in the summer sun.) But while I'm gathering our Christmas greens, Scooter continues to bound about.

Meanwhile I struggle, at least at first, trying to decide just how much to pick. I want to fill the house to overflowing, yet I don't want to rob more beauty from the outside than necessary. Soon though, when I look where I've just cut and can't tell I've taken a bit away, I snip a few more pieces.

Over the years every spring I've planted

zinnias and daisies, cosmos and snapdragons, marigolds and ageratum—all with the intention of cutting them in the summer to make lush, bountiful arrangements. Somehow, in the summer when the doors of the house are open and the constant sun is a resident from the earliest hours through half the night, all looks quite fine as it is.

But at Christmas I can't get enough color in the house. By the time I bring my garden booty inside, I have buckets full of everything there was in sight that could be cut. And the fun has just begun.

Cedar limbs must be twisted and woven together into ropes to decorate the doorways and staircase. Small bunches of boxwood must be picked off the large branches and stuck into Styrofoam pyramid forms. The woody stems of the magnolia and holly boughs must be hammered and split so they will absorb more water and keep their freshness longer.

Through this all, the kitchen floor gradually begins to look like a little forest itself. Every year I chastise myself, Next year you *must* put down paper first, and *then* begin doing the decorations. But I never remember my own admonitions until unusable twigs, loose berries, and at least an

Magnolia grandiflora leaves (above) and star magnolia blossom (below), and nandina berries (left).

*Pink roses (above),
and blue cedar
(below).*
☙

inch of discarded leaves make the floor impassable.

Every year I also make a vow to wear gloves *next* year. At the end of the day my hands are a disaster. Winter greens have thousands of sharp pinpoints. The best-smelling cedars and pines leave resin stains. And who knows what culprit splits and breaks fingernails off! My hands may look terrible, but they smell grand and have that good ache that comes from doing labor we love. They feel wonderful.

And so do I. Every year, at the end of that special decking-out-the-house day, far into the night I usually wind up, happily half-exhausted, plopped down on the bottom step where the last garland has just been looped around, and where, all alone, I sit back and admire my handiwork.

After my third try, the magnolia branches are finally standing up just the right way in my grandmother's brass coal bucket. With considerable coaxing the lustrous ivy leaves have yielded to my pleas and now gracefully and effortlessly curve in and out around my

collection of some-old, some-new silver and crystal candlesticks on the sideboard.

My eyes take in those well-put-together arrangements, but my mind's eye brings back other, simpler visions. The day has yielded so many quiet pleasures. While cutting a luscious, heavy cluster of nandina berries for the library mantel, I unexpectedly spied a tiny purple violet blossom about to open. The way the sun hit that one spot would prompt even the groundhog to come out early. And when picking a small bouquet of exquisitely fragrant star-shaped paperwhite narcissus, I noticed the pointed ears of the early-blooming crocuses peeping up through the shelter of the sandy brown oak blanket sent down by the tree above. In my Christmasy mood, I found a single powder-blue cedar berry nestled among the rich, Christmas-green needles to be the loveliest sight of all.

In the winter gardens of the South, Christmas is all around us. Among the tall long-leaf pines, the perfectly shaped, stately holly trees, and the elegant, gleaming leaves of the majestic magnolia, anyone can behold lush green boughs and an array of cheerful, seasonal colors. These remind us of Christmas. We know they will be there. We expect to be treated to these glorious sights.

But if you take the time to look more closely you will find wondrous little surprises. I think of those intimate, personal pleasures as nature's special Christmas gifts to the observing eye.

"WREATHS, AND BOUGHS, AND MISTLETOE"

∾

*I*n *The Old South*, Thomas Nelson Page wrote, "Getting the evergreens and mistletoe was the sign that Christmas had come, was really here." Old South or new, in almost every account of Southern Christmases from the pages of fiction to endearing diary entries, greens are lovingly mentioned. And rightfully so, for is there any place in a home, no matter how large or small, that is not made more beautiful by a shining touch of color or a peaceful sprig of green?

Eighteenth-century Southern colonists gathered greens to decorate their homes, churches, and shops at Christmastime, just as their ancestors had in England where rooms "were embower'd with Holly, Ivy, Cyprus, Bays, Laurel and Mistletoe." Historically, winter greens had been part of pagan celebrations and rites. Just as the Druids believed fir trees were inhabited by spirits, pre-Christian superstitions held that green boughs had magical powers, both good and bad. But when bleak, bare limbs are everywhere you look, and brown and gray color the sky and the ground, how can anyone, in any age, resist the charm of beautiful, fragrant foliage?

Certainly not the artists, poets, and musicians who long ago recorded the natural association of greenery and Christmas, both

symbols of never-ending life. The words and pictures created by great masters and small voices alike remain as fresh today as they were centuries ago. The fifteenth-century depictions of the gentle Madonna, encircled by a colorful halo of apples, oranges, lemons, pinecones, and greens, created by the Italian sculptor Luca Della Robbia are eternally poignant. And the lines written by the seventeenth-

"Why didn't I think of that?" everyone wonders when seeing the ingenious split wreath on the double doors at Middleton Plantation in Charleston, South Carolina.

∾

It only takes a few greens to decorate your window or den mantle. Add colorful fruits, splashes of red berries, subtle dried flowers and pods for texture and contrast...and of course, on the mantle, candles for a soft, romantic glow, and in no time you have a rich medley of Christmas colors.

Some call them hedge apples, others osage oranges. The little boys who play in the park near our home love to smash them. And why not? The pebble-skinned fruit of the osage tree has absolutely no use at all. It just makes the most beautifully exotic —and inexpensive— Christmas decoration imaginable. Arrangement at Liberty Hall, Kenansville, North Carolina
∞

century English poet George Witter, "Each room with ivy leaves is drest,/And every post with holly" remain forever heart-cheering, as do the universally loved lines from the Welsh Christmas carol, "Deck the halls with boughs of holly."

In the South, once the Virginia colony was established and trade begun with the Caribbean Islands, a wide variety of citrus fruits was imported around Christmastime. As early as the eighteenth century, educated European and American gentlemen were so fascinated with horticulture that when visiting foreign, tropical lands they gathered seeds and cuttings to plant in their greenhouses or "conservatories" back home. Later, in the nineteenth and early twentieth centuries, many Southern ac-

counts tell of hyacinths and lilies-of-the-valley being grown in conservatories for use in decorating "Christmas tables."

A gathering of cheerful, colorful oranges and limes, piled high in a silver epergne or white creamware bowl, are as appealing in our homes today as they were two centuries ago. These days we leave our fruit arrangements as our centerpieces, whereas in the mid-eighteenth century these treats would have been a special, once-a-year dessert.

Nowadays we have taken fruit beyond our dining room tables and sideboards to adorn the wreaths, garlands, and arrangements that dress our staircases, doorways, gates and porticos, and mantels in Christmas attire. A spray of waxy-green magnolia leaves makes a rich fringe

Christmas colors make everything more beautiful and lustrous. The fruits, greens, and berries are at home with fine porcelain and provincial faience alike. Liberty Hall, Kenansville, North Carolina

A mixture of native-grown greens, apples carried over from the fall, and fruits imported from the islands wind around the curving banister (near right). Potted orange trees (far right) imported from tropical climates to be grown in the mild-winter Southern Atlantic states are richly documented in eighteenth-century American gardeners' diaries. Tryon Palace, New Bern, North Carolina
☙

The mellow patina of family silver shines most beautifully at Christmas when generations gather. Much family silver passed through Mary Izard Middleton's line, and during the Civil War years her family home, Cedar Grove, escaped unscathed by Northern troops. Today many pieces have been returned to Middleton Plantation. Here the English epergne is filled, as it would have been in the eighteenth century, with fruit and nuts.
☙

Golden lemons and Christmas red and green apples, dried yellow yarrow, honey-brown pinecones, and a sprinkling of tiny, beadlike holly clusters interwoven against a variety of evergreens create a robust and joyful Christmas mantel decoration. The presence of the violin fills the room with the promise of Christmas carols once the guests arrive.

Liberty Hall, Kenansville, North Carolina

∽

The Vanderbilts did everything at Christmas on a grand scale. Crimson-red poinsettias add the perfect splash of color to the Gothic-style conservatory of the Biltmore House in Asheville, North Carolina (above). Topiary deer (right) stand among a fantasy poinsettia forest on the table in the baronial dining room.
~

around plump red apples placed in fanlight-windowed doorways. Thorny-tipped pinecones, fragrant long-needled pine boughs, bright yellow lemons, oranges and red berries, and diminutive lady apples fit snugly into small window boxes.

Southerners have always been creative in their use of natural greens and flowers for the Christmas holidays. In fact, the single greatest gift the South has made to everyone's continuing Christmas cheer was the introduction of the poinsettia to America well over 150 years ago.

In 1825, Joel Roberts Poinsett, a Charlestonian who was both secretary of war and America's first ambassador to Mexico, became charmed by a "weed" the Mexicans called Flower of the Holy Night. Poinsett brought the crimson-leafed plant to America with him, where it was named poinsettia in his honor.

No other Christmas plant is as appealing as the showy poinsettia that now comes in white, pink, and even variegated red-and-white varieties that look like sponge-painted crepe paper. And its uses at Christmas are limitless. At Opryland, in Nashville, Tennessee, an opulent, multilayered "poinsettia tree" towers so high it almost touches the vaulted ceiling. In a tiny nineteenth-century clapboard church in rural northwestern Texas, two red poinsettias are the sole Christmas decorations on the altar.

Another beautiful Southern Christmas flower is the enchanting camellia, which grows in abundance from southern Virginia to Florida and points west. Though camellias have been in the South since the eighteenth century, they are delicate shrubs. A sudden frost or a continuously cold winter will kill the buds and turn the open blos-

soms a dingy brown. Yet during those years when all the conditions are perfect and our camellias are at their peak bloom, I often hear people unfamiliar with these shrubs say that their fragile, almost ethereal, ruffled petals symbolize the refinement and graciousness of the old South.

To me, December's camellia bush is nature's already-decorated outdoor Christmas tree. Its blossoms—whether half unfurled or fully opened—are as showy in the bright sunshine as any string of lights or profusion of Christmas balls. And when cut

Poinsettias were first used for Christmas decorations in Charleston, South Carolina. Here, in the 1828 Edmondston-Alston House, 1990s pink poinsettias are at home beneath an eighteenth-century ancestral portrait.

A virtual merry-go-round of varicolored almond-filled cornucopias (below) surrounds the Gorham coin silver tea service, heart-shaped cookies, and picture-perfect ribbon candy—all essential ingredients for a proper Victorian Christmas tea in New Orleans. The cornucopias were made from instructions in the household books of the day (right). Gallier House, New Orleans, Louisiana

Versatile amaryllis blossoms (far left) are used like any cut flower in this Sevres vase, along with lark-spur, snapdragons, Queen Anne's lace, and seasonal cedar and pine. Bragg-Mitchell House, Mobile, Alabama

"Busy hands make happy hearts" the Victorians believed. Well-heeled nine-teenth-century ladies worked hundreds of tiny diamondlike beads onto metallic threads to create intricate everlasting beaded flowers (left). Gallier House, New Orleans, Louisiana

A golden carpet of ginkgo leaves covers the Grand Crescent Lawn at the circa 1855 Bragg-Mitchell House (far left). This sight, one of nature's many seasonal gifts, inspired Patrice Baur to create silk ginkgo leaves for packages (left) placed beneath the gold and crystal Christmas tree.

A Gift to the Reader
HANDCRAFTED
CAMELLIAS

If you don't have live camellias to use inside, you can make long-lasting paper ones for your tree, packages, or Christmas dinner table. You will need crepe paper (I prefer white), small white paper doilies, green leaves bought at a craft shop, florist wire and tape, ribbon, scissors, and wire cutters.

Lay the crepe paper out with the grain of the paper running top to bottom. Cut out fourteen to eighteen heart-shaped petals. Pull gently at the sides of each petal. This makes each petal less stiff, more flowerlike. Wrap one petal around a single florist wire and secure the bottom half inch with florist tape. Arrange four green leaves around the stem and tape each one in place. Next arrange five petals around the stem, securely taping each one.

Continue adding petals in this manner in graduated rows until the flower is as full as you wish. (Once you've made two or three, you'll know how many petals you want each flower to have.) Push the wire stem through a paper doily and then fluff up the petals and leaves. From beneath, wrap floral tape around the wire and curl it into a loose, attractive "corkscrew" tail.

Bows or streamers of colorful ribbon can be added if desired, especially if these are to be used as table decorations.

and taken inside, a single camellia spray or two will grace any room with subtle beauty.

Much bolder and more traditional Southern winter greens have long been used in imaginative ways to decorate our homes both inside and out. In a nineteenth-century Mississippi diary, the writer described suspending "great bunches of holly and magnolia, of pine and mistletoe" from the hall, dining room, and drawing room ceilings. Though her mention of the drawing room lends a formal note to the description, in Tifton, Georgia, green garlands hung on the front porch of a country house were as unpretentious and as "at home" as green ribbons tied around a Christmas gift.

In short, there are no rules for using the native Southern vegetation that grows all around us at Christmastime. The shrubs, trees, vines, and flowers supply us with an endless variety of colors and textures that never fail to brighten our homes.

We, like our Southern ancestors of the eighteenth and nineteenth centuries, can express our own Christmas moods with boughs and sprigs, blossoms and berries. We can bring drama, serenity, even humor and whimsy to every corner of our homes as our welcoming decorations announce "Christmas is really here."

On my Christmas journey through the South, beauty was everywhere. Decorations on doors, in windows, around stair steps, above portraits, even in tucked-away and otherwise unnoticeable niches turned every

Drooping vine leaves and their twisted limbs add charm and color to this portrait of Arthur and Mary Izard Middleton and their son Henry (left), painted by Benjamin West in 1771, which has a Christmasy look about it. Over the years family members have affectionately referred to the painting as "the Holy Family."
∾

Camellias have traveled far. In the late eighteenth century, when the French botanist Andre Michaux was in America to collect plants for the king of France, he introduced four camellias to Henry Middleton. Lush, exotic camellias have been the glory of the Middleton gardens outside Charleston ever since (above and left).
∾

*W*ho needs greens when swags of brown pinecones gathered and tied by bright red bows can do the job (above)? Beauregard-Keyes House, New Orleans, Louisiana

∾

*E*verlasting live oak trees (right) shade a boxwood and fruit garland on the scroll-and-acanthus-motif iron gate at the Tryon Palace in New Bern, North Carolina.

∾

44

scene into little Christmas cards. They were personal greetings—sometimes from friends, other times from people I would never meet.

Each decoration expressed something dear and special about the person who had made it. Time and thought had gone into every wreath, spray, or arrangement. Every place I looked, unspoken messages of care and enthusiasm peeped through.

The patience it took to tie a bow that certain way or the running around on a Saturday morning or late at night that had to be done to find just the right color trim were labors of love. The extra effort and trouble that were necessary to get the decorations high above a doorway or upon a high chandelier were well worth it. For there is no more happy or generous way to share the spirit of Christmas than to make a thing of beauty for all to behold.

Enjoy these vignettes we gathered in private homes and public museums, cozy bed-and-breakfasts and grand hotels, on walks through busy city parks and quiet, deep woods—all places where our hearts were warmed and spirits lifted by the grand variety of seasonal decorations we found in the lovely South.

At Christmastime, the porch of this nineteenth-century house in Savannah is dressed in stars and stripes, reminding us of America's early patriotic spirit.

❧

These looped paper garlands (right) are as much fun to make today as they were during Victorian days at Middleton Place in South Carolina. Evergreen garlands (below) are draped about the Victorian parlor of the Gallier House in New Orleans. In the 1850s, dried foliage sprayed gold, like that shown in the trumpet-shaped cobalt blue vases, was highly fashionable. ❧

Ribbon was expensive and used sparingly until the later nineteenth century. Swirls of red ribbon woven among kumquats, magnolia leaves, and holly berries enhance the rich color and distinctive graining of the small mahogany sideboard. De Mesa-Sanchez House, Saint Augustine, Florida

Graceful garlands wrap the porches and balconies of the Hall House, in Salisbury, North Carolina, in seasonal grandeur.

*T*he owners of the Ballastone Inn capture Savannah's centuries-old seaport history in their Christmas door-dressing. Garlands of fishing nets are sprinkled with shells, starfish, and fruits—reminders of the treats brought by ships from the islands in bygone years.
∾

During the eighteenth century, fruits were too rare to use outdoors, but today we can freely use them (left and below).

Wild native field grasses add interest and surprise to an otherwise traditionally green and red door decoration (left and above).

Bell-shaped pears, grapes, and small lady apples enhance this wreath (far left top).

The cragged rock walls of the Grove Park Inn in Asheville, North Carolina (near left top), provide a stunning background for this Christmas wreath, with its own red ribbon wrapping.

The decorations along the quaint streets of Colonial Williamsburg must be natural and native to the region. Turkey feathers add an imaginative touch to this wreath (far left bottom).

Bright green hedge apples, golden oranges, and kumquats are seasonally colorful against a Williamsburg wreath of deep-green boxwood (near left bottom).

We came upon this eye-catching 1990s Texas Christmas greeting (right) in the parking lot of a Mexican restaurant in Beaumont.

Christmas Trees

"PAPA'S CHRISTMAS TREE"

"Christmas is a magic time," my grandfather, or Papa as I called him, always said. So on his Christmas evergreen he hung summertime oranges, apples, lemons, and when they were available, a lime or two. Everyone knew fruit couldn't really grow on a fir, cedar, or pine tree, especially in the winter. Yet each year for just a few days we could pretend. We put reality aside and entered a "magic time" when miracles and mysteries needed no explanation.

As a little girl in the late 1940s, I happily left the real world the week before Christmas as my parents and I drove down the main street of Danville,

Virginia. Usually it was close to dusk. Other chores had taken up most of the day. At last the time had come to choose our very own, special tree from the assortment of evergreens the farmers had brought in on wooden-slatted wagons hitched to their work-weary cars. Few could afford to have both a truck

In the nineteenth century, the farmers brought Christmas greens to the city market square in Alexandria, Virginia.
∾

and a car in those days. But I never noticed the rusting cars then. For in my mind's eye the scent of freshly cut cedar, the nip in the air, and of course, the magic of Christmas transformed the asphalt pavement into a gray cobblestone street, the cars into sleighbell-harnessed horses, and the rubber-wheeled wagons into bright red sleighs—all straight from the Christmas cards Mother had begun addressing a few days before.

While Mother and I watched, Daddy would take tree after tree off the wagon, shak-

ing out each one for inspection, until we made our choice. Then while our tree was being tied across the roof of our car and the trunk packed to overflowing with holly boughs and pine tree limbs needed to make the front door wreath and decorate the mantel and staircase, I picked out a sprig of mistletoe with a heavy cluster of iridescent berries to hang on the kissing ball.

All the way home we talked about how we had chosen the *perfect* tree. But once it was standing straight in the wooden stand Daddy had nailed together, some imperfection we'd missed would always show up. The limbs might be too bushy around the bottom, or perhaps the tree had a flat side. There never was any doubt, though, that the tree would be tall enough to scrape the top of the living room ceiling. Daddy had seen to that by measuring the tree's height against his own almost six-foot-tall frame. And what did it matter that the tree might not be perfectly formed, for once it was dressed in red and green and frosted with silver icicles, we knew we really had picked the best tree—next best after Papa's tree that is.

By the 1950s my grandparents had moved. Now our tree could stand alone without being compared to Papa's tree. It's a good thing, too, because over the years, as I grew up, our Christmas trees grew a little shorter, a little smaller. Oh, the tree was always the same size. It's just that as I grew taller I could put decorations on higher limbs that the year before had been out of reach, but not out of sight. Thinking back, I'm awfully glad my grandparents' majestic trees will never shrink the way our Christmas tree did each year.

It was also during the 1950s that I began to accumulate my motley collection of Christmas tree ornaments. "Theme trees" were popular about that time and everyone had to have the newest-fashioned Christmas tree. Mother bought the bright pink glass balls—today I usually hang those toward the back of the tree—the year after we saw the all-pink Christmas trees in Pennsylvania Station. I believe that Mamie Eisenhower was responsible for that fleeting fad.

And the clusters of gold and silver pinecones that I will lay among the branches of our Christmas tree this year date from about 1955. Those were the Christmases when we spray-painted everything in sight. Magnolia leaves, pine boughs, holly berries, and the plastic sleds and reindeer left over from the late 1940s were given a shiny, metallic coat. I remember that the following year we took the Styrofoam balls we had frosted only twelve months earlier, dipped them in glue, and rolled them in pink, blue, and gold sequins. Just a few of those go a long way on today's Christmas tree!

In my teenage years, the mid- and late-1950s, I pored through magazines, faithfully following the latest Christmas colors and styles. But my "traditional" family called a halt to having a "fashionable" Christmas the year modernism came in. Somehow, one-dimensional black Christmas-tree mobiles and red, spiked "porcupine" balls looked singularly out of place against the mellow patina of early American walnut and cherry antiques. Though

my best high school friend and I did cover some cut-out angular cardboard Christmas trees in whimsical "Space Santa" wrapping paper, I haven't come upon those in recent years.

Most of my Christmas-tree ornaments date from the 1960s and 1970s—those years when we were setting up our first apartment and home, and when our now-grown children, Langdon and Joslin (whom we nicknamed Joli), were small. As a newlywed, my Christmases were alternately spent one year with my parents, one year with my in-laws. When I visited with my parents, Mother and I would inevitably splurge on a new ornament or two we couldn't resist during the course of our normal Christmas shopping.

Thank goodness, by then, whether traditional Christmases had become popular again or whether we were both mature enough to follow our hearts instead of fashion, we chose timeless Christmas themes. One year Mother took home a fuzzy squirrel eating an acorn encased in a glass ball. She has always loved all

Even if oranges and apples can't grow on evergreens, using a fruit tree as a Christmas tree truly captures the symbolism of the tree of life. The egg-shaped kumquats lend cheerful dots of color to this New Orleans 1850s Christmas tree.

creatures great and small. The ball first cracked and then broke sometime along the way, but the squirrel remains a permanent fixture on our tree. Another year I bought a porcelain angel. So far, miraculously, even her wings are chip-free—but I know that can't last forever.

When the children came along I wisely moved to wooden and papier-mâché ornaments: miniature nutcrackers, little red engines, dolls in colonial dress. Even today, though the children are young adults in their early twenties, those ornaments that bring back memories of their younger years are my favorites. And so ours is primarily a perennial children's tree, regardless of the newest fashions I see in the trim-a-tree shops of every department store. Around the bottom of the tree I cluster the stuffed animals the children have accumulated over the years. From one-eared kittens and mangey pups to a green-felt Kermit, these old friends come out of the closets and down from high shelves to bring smiles to everyone who sees them.

Could it really have been some forty-odd years ago that I drove down the main street of that sleepy southside Virginia town to bring home a Christmas tree? How many changes have occurred in such a seemingly short time. Today I wander among the blue spruces, fraser firs, and Scotch pines strung along the brightly lighted Christmas-tree lot. These are perfectly shaped, cultivated trees, painstakingly pruned by professional tree farmers. They have no bushy bottoms or flat sides. On each hangs a tag with the tree's exact height boldly printed in black magic marker.

Funny, I never knew what kind of tree we had. I don't even know how high the ceilings were in the house where I grew up. Deep in my heart I long for the simplicity and innocence of those bygone days. But I don't despair, for once I get my picture-perfect tree home, I dress it in memories of past Christmases and live each year over again.

That's the magic of Christmas.

Old family decorations blend beautifully with brand-new ornaments (left) I couldn't resist buying as mementos of the many wonderful museums and restorations we visited throughout the South.

Small artificial Christmas trees known as feather trees were bought for a dollar at the turn of the century. They were made from goose or turkey feathers that were stripped from their quills, dyed green, and wrapped around wooden dowels. This old feather tree and its glass ornaments still in the original box at the Baxter-Henley House in Jonesborough, Tennessee, have been lovingly preserved for almost a century.

"AMONG THE BRANCHES"

❧

You really don't have to hang any decorations on a Christmas tree to make it beautiful. Its rich green color, heady fragrance, graceful boughs, and towering presence are all that are needed to fill any room with seasonal beauty and festive Christmas spirit. If your Christmas tree is the traditional evergreen, that is.

Whoever heard of using a kumquat tree for a Christmas tree? They did in New Orleans in the 1850s. A large water oak? Wilmington, North Carolina, has decked out a seventy-five-foot-tall water oak with lights and Spanish moss as its official city Christmas tree for years. A prickly holly? A wax myrtle? Since their nineteenth-century beginnings, Southern Christmas trees have come in all shapes, sizes, and varieties.

Finding so many creative ideas for Southern Christmas trees recorded through the years, I couldn't help but wonder if anyone had identified the origin

The wax myrtle is little more than a shrub, but a few candles, paper cornucopias, crocheted snowflakes, and cookies decorated with paper designs called "scraps" that were glued on with egg whites, turn it into a full fledged Christmas tree. The eggshells among the wax myrtle limbs symbolize birth. During the nineteenth century, eggs were carefully cracked and the shells painted, trimmed, and gilded. Gallier House, New Orleans, Louisiana

❧

and date of the first Southern Christmas tree.

I thought the question was a simple one, but the more I searched, the more elusive the answer became. Some days my desk was piled so high with books and reference materials I could hardly find the phone to call the next museum curator or Christmas specialist whom I thought would know the answer.

In dusty, often dog-eared books written by nineteenth-century Southern authors I found wonderful references to ageless myths associating trees with Christmas celebrations. In *Memories of an Old-Time Tarheel*, the autobiography of Kemp Plummer Battle, president of the University of North Carolina from 1876 to 1891, he mentions that the first Christmas tree was a cherry tree that bowed down to give shade and fruit to a weary and hungry Virgin Mary.

But historians who know much more than I do tell us that the Christmas tree really began before Christ's birth. It seems that during pagan times, trees were worshipped because they were thought to be inhabited by unseen spirits. (If you've ever seen tree branches move mysteriously in a windless night, you too may believe in tree spirits.) The Puritans later used this and other pagan associations as justification for keeping December 25 stark and barren. And indeed, the apples, cakes, nuts, and meat hung on the branches as gifts to the pagan gods—especially at the winter solstice so near to the Christmas celebration—are remarkably akin to the apples, cookies, and nuts the Victorians hung on their Christmas trees many centuries later.

Yet many centuries before the stoical Puritans took the joy out of Christmas, the tree was part of Christmas celebrations throughout Europe. In a widely performed medieval play about Adam and Eve, one of the simple props was a fir tree hung with apples. During the same time, a popular superstition was that evergreens would scare the devil away. And in the eighth century, a gentle, Anglican saint, St. Boniface, dedicated a fir tree to the Holy Child on Christmas Eve.

By the sixteenth century, trees "for Christmas" could be bought in several areas of Europe. During this same century, legend says that the great religious reformer Martin Luther was so

touched by the resplendent stars in the clear December sky that he rushed home and put candles on his children's tree to show them that Christ was the light of the world.

No one knows whether or not this really happened, of course, but in 1845 (Luther had died in 1546), the German-born artist Carl A. Schwerdgeburth painted a sentimental, mid-nineteenth-century depiction of Martin Luther and his family gathered around a candle-lighted Christmas tree. Three years later, in 1848, an etching of Queen Victoria, her German prince consort, Albert, and their children admiring their tabletop Christmas tree appeared in the *Illustrated London News*. In 1850 the American magazine *Godey's Lady's Book* printed a slightly different version of the same scene.

These two depictions of Martin Luther and Queen Victoria around their candle-lighted family trees had untold influence on Christmas celebrations. Who could resist the charm of a tree, a symbol of ongoing life, cheerfully decorated to bring delight to a family celebration? And so for most people, not just in the

Opulence, deep rich colors, more and more bows! Tinsel and glitter make this re-created 1885 Christmas tree in the Smith-McDowell House in Asheville, North Carolina, a wonder to behold. The table is especially draped for the season in a complementary gold and purple (two favorite Victorian colors) skirt. The Victorians loved tiers of billowing fabric.

ington (a Virginian, remember) and his troops came upon Hessian soldiers celebrating around a candle-lighted tree, a tradition they had brought to America with them. Though the story seems plausible, no documentation of this event survives. Knowing how Virginians loved their Christmastime, I tend to think that if the story were really true, Washington as well as many of his soldiers would have added this colorful and festive ornament to their own holiday celebrations.

There is another, widely known account of an early Southern Christmas tree—this one from the 1840s in Williamsburg, Virginia. In 1928, Mrs. Martha Vandergrift, then ninety-five years old, told the *Richmond News Leader* the thrill of being present when Charles Frederick Erners Minnigerode, a young professor of Greek and Latin at William and Mary College, cut an evergreen in the woods and presented it to Judge Nathaniel B. Tucker's young children.

"Supreme excitement reigned in the Tucker family on that Christmas day in Williamsburg," Mrs. Vandergrift recalled. "Other children of the neighborhood were invited in, and they danced and shouted as the candles were lit one by one. There were no devices to clip the candles to the tree, and it was done by twisting pieces of wire. Tinsel and glass balls were not to be bought in Virginia in 1845, so Dr. Minnigerode had cut out bits of brightly colored papers, and a gilded star was hung above the branches. When the tree had been admired and Christmas gifts exchanged, the

South but throughout America, the Christmas tree as a time-honored family tradition began in the 1850s.

There are earlier stories of Southern Christmas trees that should be told. One goes that on Christmas night, 1776, General Wash-

This cheerful, toy-laden floor-to-ceiling tree (right) could have stepped out of the pages of the December 1860 Godey's Lady's Book into the Georgia Dining Room for the Yuletide celebration at the Henry Francis du Pont Winterthur Museum. Commercial Christmas ornaments were not readily available until the 1880s, yet the colorful ribbon gatherings are as eye-catching as the tinsel roping that later became all the rage.
❧

Poinsettias and angels made from dried corn shucks add a bit of Kentucky folk art to a grapevine Christmas tree (opposite).
❧

Nine tiers of Christmas poinsettias, like beautiful, textured damask, create a glorious floral Christmas tree at Dunleith in Natchez, Mississippi.
∾

her students arranged a wonderful surprise for the girls who, during that time, did not go home for Christmas.

"When the doors were flung open on Christmas night, and we marched in singing a carol, we beheld a holly tree reaching from floor to ceiling ablaze with lights and hung with gifts for everyone. A thing of light and beauty and loving kindness! The tree so planted in the heart of Saint Mary's took root and still lives to bring merriment to the girls of today," Emilie Smedes Holmes remembered many years later.

Christmas trees are such an accepted part of our twentieth-century Christmas celebrations that we would think a young girl from an educated and affluent family would have seen her first Christmas tree before she was sixteen or eighteen years old. But we must realize that opulent, richly adorned Christmas trees really didn't appear until the 1850s, and even then, Christmas trees weren't prevalent until the turn of the century. In my 1990s travels throughout the South, when I would talk to much older people living in country areas, time after time I was told, "I saw my first Christmas tree when I was ten or twelve years old." That's why I was so surprised, and wonderfully excited to learn of this very early, back-country reference to a Southern Christmas tree.

As early as 1801 at Spring Place Mission in northcentral Georgia, white missionaries brought Christmas to the Cherokee Indian nation. In a little-known diary now in the archives at Old Salem, in Salem, North Carolina, a December 21, 1805, entry written in

older people led the young in singing hymns and carols."

Apparently other German teachers introduced Christmas trees to young Southerners during the mid-nineteenth century. In 1879, at Saint Mary's College in Raleigh, North Carolina, a German *fraulein* the same age as many of

German by one of the missionaries describes a three-mile cart ride to fetch a Christmas tree. The following year they did the same.

These diary entries make us wonder. If the custom of the Christmas tree was known so early in the wilderness country of northcentral Georgia, where else must it have been celebrated? The answers, the references, lie in the countless diaries and letters written in the early eighteen hundreds. Most of these were long ago discarded, but many are still packed away—whether in archives and libraries, or trunks and desk drawers—waiting to be read again.

Yet we can become so caught up in our abundant, glittering twentieth-century Christmases that we easily forget the lovely simplicity of early Southern Christmases. When visiting many restorations, museums, and historical homes—those predating the 1850s—I would hear many tourists ask, "But where's the Christmas tree?" We must remember that when historic homes are decked out in Christmas finery in eighteenth- and early nineteenth-

This whimsical tree is at home in the spacious front hall of Green Leaves, a stately mansion built in Natchez, in 1838. Virginia Morrison started her unique bear tree almost twenty-five years ago. The oldest bear dates back to 1903 and belonged to Virginia's mother.

*A*ny niche can house
a Christmas tree, like
the corner cubbyhole
(right) at the Grove
Park Inn in Asheville,
North Carolina.

*R*ed, white, and blue
stars and stripes on
this tree (above) made
by Fay Papi in Fred-
ericksburg, Virginia,
are Christmasy and
patriotic.

The gate is always open at the base of this New Mexican tree, where native American dolls stand watch. "New Mexico is my spiritual home," Marilyn Whelpley says, and so each year in her Savannah home she dresses a small theme tree with various Hopi kachina dolls interspersed with colored lights and halos (left).

❧

Sterling silver ornaments lovingly collected year after year hold special memories of Christmases past (above).

❧

A Gift to the Reader
TUSSIE-MUSSIES

*T*he art of making a tussie-mussie is as simple as gathering a few flowers in your hand. Dried, paper, silk, or real flowers can be used, but first take into account the size you wish the arrangement to be and whether the stems can be kept in water—which they seldom can be. Therefore tussie-mussies to be laid among the limbs of a tree or for long-term use are best made from dried or artificial blossoms. Also, since large blooms overpower a small bouquet, delicate flowers are usually preferred. You do want a variety of textures, colors, and shapes though. A combination of miniature pinecones, dried baby's breath, artificial berries, and diminutive silk flowers yield an interesting, colorful seasonal gathering. The pictures of tussie-mussies in these pages should give you several different ideas.

To make a delicate tussie-mussie, cup one of your hands as if it were a vase by making a ring or circle with your thumb and first finger and then enclosing your other fingers beneath this ring. In the center of your small "hand-vase" place the largest, prettiest, most showy or colorful of your flowers. Now surround this with the other blossoms, berries, or foliage you have selected, saving leafy foliage or spiky stems for the outer ring. The size of

your natural "hand-vase" should hold just the right number of stems to make a graceful cluster. When you are satisfied with the arrangement, wrap the stems securely with floral tape. Your tussie-mussie is now ready to be "dressed" by sticking it through a small paper doily, wrapping it in a profusion of ribbon streamers, or placing it in a small vase, glass, or one of the silver or porcelain holders made especially for these arrangements.

Or you may want to make a fabric container. A simple linen holder can be used throughout the year by changing the tussie-mussie in it to suit the season—or you may select a particularly Christmasy fabric to match your decorating scheme. Cut out a circle, approximately 5 or 6 inches in diameter. Finish the border of the circle to your liking (a simple hemstitch will do, or you can add lace or ribbon) and fold the two sides across the front so one slightly overlaps the other, making a cone shape. Stitch these laps together and you have an instant tussie-mussie holder.

Theme trees were as popular in the nineteenth century as they are today. Ribbon garlands weave around diminutive bisque dolls and rosebud tussie-mussies on this tabletop tree (left and above) in the parlor at Tulip Grove in Nashville, Tennessee.

❧

century fashion, Christmas trees will not be part of their decoration.

On my journey to chronicle Southern Christmases, the best example I found that shows the distinct difference between the decorations, even as late as the 1830s, from the decorations of the 1850s was in Nashville, Tennessee. There, only a few yards apart, are two houses you can visit: The Hermitage, President Andrew Jackson's home; and Tulip Grove, the home of President Jackson's nephew, Andrew Jackson Donelson. Both homes were built in the 1830s, and The Hermitage is decorated as it would have been at Christmas in the 1830s.

Simple cedar wreaths are hung at the windows. In the library, stockings for the children in the house (President Jackson had no children himself) are placed upon the sofa as family accounts tell us they were. Upstairs, laid out on a grand tester bed, I saw a few silks and laces that would have been Christmas presents brought inland from New Orleans on the boats that traveled the Mississippi. But there is no Christmas tree.

For more than twenty years, the two-story-tall tree at Wakefield-Scearce in Shelbyville, Kentucky, has been decorated with ten thousand ornaments, attracting visitors from across the country.

࿋

There's a lot of "Southern" in this tree (right and far right) that blends sentiment and whimsy in Saint Simons Island, Georgia. The fraser fir comes from North Carolina, the decorations from Texas, and family members come from all over. The famous Southern greeting, "Happy Yule, Y'all" captures the humor of a Texas Christmas. Davis-Aikins-Burres Cottage.

Marilyn Whelpley's Savannah, Georgia, Christmas tree (right) takes over a month to decorate. On her tree are hundreds of ornaments from around the world.

At Dunleith, one of Natchez's many National Historic Landmarks, the profusion of tiny clear lights and almost all-white Victorian-style ornaments (far right) create a light, snowlike greeting to the guests staying in the bed-and-breakfast quarters.

On the traditional Chrismon tree, hand-made white and gold Chrismons symbolize eternal life. The name Chrismon *comes from the combination of* CHRIST *and* MONogram. *The Chrismons are simple copies of Christian symbols, both traditional and new. From this inspired idea conceived by Frances Kipps Spencer, the Chrismon tree is now a tradition throughout the Christian world.*
Kaye Anne and Bill Aikins, Durham, North Carolina

A Gift to the Reader
TRIQUETRA AND CIRCLE

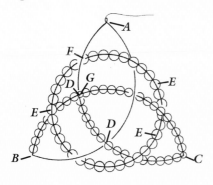

Materials: *6- and 8-mm silver beads; 10-mm pearls; #20 silver-colored wire; #18 or #20 gold- or copper-colored wire; #30 wire*

Directions: *To bring the pattern to scale, redraw it with the circle having a diameter of 3 ¾ inch and each semicircular arc having a diameter of 5 ⅛ inch. Make a loop A from the figure at the end of a length of #20 silver wire. After the loop, bend the wire to the AB semicircle, the first arc of the triquetra. String 24 8-mm silver beads on the wire to make the AB arc. With needle-nosed pliers bend the wire at B (leaving ¼ inch play of beads on the wire to allow space for the joining of the arcs after all of them are strung). Shape the next arc, BC, of the triquetra to conform to the shape of the pattern. Run another 24 beads on the wire, bend the wire at point C. Make the third arc, CA, in the same way. At the end of the arc, make a loop in the wire to fit over the first loop at A. Cut off the excess wire. Lap the arcs over and under each other as they are shown on the pattern. With #30 wire, fasten the two end loops together; the leftover wire is the hanger. Wrap #30 wire around the two wires of the triquetra where they cross over each other at the three D points. Count the beads in each arc so that each side of the central triad equals each of the other sides.*

For the circle, make a tiny loop in the end of a 16-inch length of #18 or #20 gold- or copper-colored wire. Shape the wire to form a circle with a diameter of 3 ¾ inch. String the wire circle with 10-mm pearls. At the end, make another loop in the wire to fit over the first loop. Cut off the excess wire.

Shape the triquetra so that it flows over and under the pearl circle as it is shown on the pattern. With #20 wire, attach an 8-mm bead to make the point at the end of the arc of the triquetra as shown at C. Fasten a pearl at each of the other two points. If necessary, wire a 6- or 8-mm bead over the crossover D points to hide the attachment wires as shown at G. Weave the pearl circle in and out of the triquetra. Position the joining loops of the circle directly behind a wire of the triquetra, F. Wire the circle ends together with #30 wire. Use that same wire to fasten the F loops to the back of the triquetra. When the triquetra undulates properly over and under the circle, this attachment alone will hold the two figures in position; however the circle may be wired to the triquetra at several other points if desired.

The directions for making this Chrismon are given in this book with the generous cooperation of the Ascension Lutheran Church. Chrismons may only be made for personal use or to be given as gifts, never to be sold. Pattern books are available by writing to Ascension Lutheran Church, 314 West Main Street, Danville, VA 24541.

This present-filled Christmas tree, high on the columned porch of a downtown Savannah, Georgia, antebellum home— now converted to an office building—offers a refreshing moment of Christmas cheer to all who glimpse it.

At Tulip Grove, though, where the house is decorated as it would have been in the early 1850s, in the parlor is a tabletop tree much like the one pictured in *Godey's Lady's Book* in 1850. Lace, ribbons, toys, and tussie-mussies are nestled among the tree's limbs. Andrew Jackson Donelson, who was President Jackson's White House secretary, had seen such trees when he was ambassador to Prussia. He was undoubtedly one of many visitors to Europe who brought the charm of the Christmas tree to the South upon returning to America.

Once they were introduced, trees became very popular, especially in the urban shipping centers of the South. In 1851, the Charleston *Courier* reported that the ladies in town prepared a "brilliant" Christmas tree for the famous Swedish Nightingale soprano, Jenny Lind, who was visiting at Christmastime.

And in the deep South, Susan Dabney Smedes recalled that during Christmas in the 1850s at Burleigh Plantation in Mississippi,

"Sometimes, not often, there was a Christmas-tree—on one occasion one for the colored Sunday-school."

Whether the tradition spread from first-hand accounts of Christmas trees seen in Europe, illustrations and literature published in America, or reports of the first White House Christmas tree in 1853, by the 1850s Christmas trees were found throughout the South. But a Southern Christmas traveler in those nineteenth-century days certainly couldn't expect to find a "picture-perfect" Christmas tree every place he visited. In fact, he would have found that people simply used native trees—whatever was available—to add beauty and decoration to their holidays.

Dr. John Carmichael Jenkins, a wealthy Natchez, Mississippi, plantation owner, wrote in his 1845 to 1852 diaries about the large pine Christmas trees where everyone gathered for Christmas presents. But just down the Mississippi River from Natchez, a small wax myrtle was the first documented New Orleans Christmas tree. In fact, during the mid-nineteenth century New Orleanians decorated Japanese plum trees, althea bushes, even long-leaf pine trees for Christmas.

Just as many different types of trees were used as Christmas trees, so the decorations hung upon them were limited only by the family's imagination and pocketbook. In the nineteenth century the branches of the most lavish Christmas trees were laden with rosy-cheeked dolls, toy drums, picture books, and store-bought games. A 1935 recollection de-

A CHRISTMAS GARDEN

We never gave it a name, but every Christmas for as long as I can remember, our family has made a "Christmas garden." No, our Christmas garden isn't a host of poinsettia, amaryllis, or even early-blooming camellias. In fact, until I began writing this book, I didn't know it was a Christmas garden. Under our tree we assemble a conglomeration of items, from the ten-cent store variety to our treasured, and very elegant, Royal Doulton "Christmas Morn" figurine. There are the miniature cottages Clauston has given me as special no-reason-at-all surprise presents, the children's stuffed animals (our family's own Peaceable Kingdom), an oversize wooden Nutcracker I bought on sale because he had a broken jaw, and the mismatched remains of a Nativity scene Mother assembled in the 1930s.

But if we had lived in Baltimore, Maryland, we would have called our under-the-tree scene a Christmas garden and it would have included a train set weaving its way around a fanciful, nonsensical landscape. Or had we lived in Winston-Salem, North Carolina, we would have referred to our scene as a putz, the term the Moravians used for these Christmas arrangements.

Regardless of its name, the tradition of putting a family's toys—and my cottages are certainly my grown-up toys—under the Christmas tree, whether it is tabletop or floor-to-ceiling, has long been an endearing custom in many Southern homes.

A Gift to the Reader
CROCHETED
SNOWFLAKES

My husband's aunt gave us our first crocheted snowflakes in the 1960s. Of course they are now being commercially sold, but I have always kept her patterns in the box with our handmade snowflakes. Here is one of her patterns.

Starting at the center, chain 10. Join with slip stitch to form ring. 1st round: Chain 4, 2 treble in ring, chain 9, single crochet in 7th, chain from hook. Large picot made.

* (Chain 7, single crochet in 5th chain from hook) twice; (chain 4, single crochet in same place where last single crochet was made) twice; Chain 7, single crochet in 5th chain from hook, chain 9, single crochet in 7th chain from hook—another large picot made.

Chain 2, slip stitch in top of last treble made, treble in ring, chain 4 single stitch in ring. One spoke completed.

Chain 4, 2 treble in ring, chain 6, join with slip stitch in last large picot made; chain 3, skip 3 chain preceding joining slip stitch just made, single crochet in next chain. Repeat from * 4 times more; (chain 7, single crochet in 5th chain from hook) twice; (chain 4, single crochet in same place where last single crochet was made) twice; chain 7, single crochet in 5th chain from hook, chain 6, slip stitch in first large picot on first spoke, chain 3, skip 3 chain preceding joining slip stitch just made, single crochet in next chain, chain 2, single stitch in top of last treble made, treble in ring, chain 4, slip stitch in ring—6 spokes. Break off and fasten.

To make the hanger for snowflakes, chain 25, slip stitch in tip of any spoke, chain 25. Join first chain of first chain-25. Break off and fasten.

To make snowflakes hold their shape, use 3 tablespoons each of water and instant laundry starch. Saturate each snowflake and squeeze out excess. Stretch and pin the snowflake into correct shape on a waxpaper-covered padded surface. Dry thoroughly before removing.

picted "grandmother's nineteenth-century tree" in North Carolina this way: "Everything; dolls, horns, drums, little chairs—no matter how awkward and ungainly—was suspended among the branches."

During the nineteenth century, trees were put up after the children had gone to bed so when they first saw the tree on Christmas morning it was filled with their gifts. But in addition to the toys were those Christmas-tree ornaments that would remain on the tree after the gifts had been eagerly taken off the tree.

Christmas-tree ornaments in the 1850s were mostly handmade. Inexpensive tin cookie cutters were available by then, and cookies in playful animal shapes as well as Santa Claus and human figures joined white popcorn and brightly colored paper-chain garlands on the tree limbs. Nuts and seed pods gathered from beneath the primeval trees that lined the dirt streets of Southern towns and villages were also used, either in their natural state or after they were brightly painted, varnished, or gilded.

For those families to whom finer and more costly materials were available, nineteenth-century magazines provided both how-

In Saint Augustine, Florida, a tree at the Flagler Hospital celebrates the city's Spanish heritage. Clusters of gold and silver-threaded floral sprays, gold mesh ribbon, silver angels, and little glass globes adorn this tribute to the past.
~

to instructions and illustrations for fancier tree ornaments. Crocheted snowflakes, lace and ribbon-trimmed cornucopias, and eggshells dressed the trees in wealthy homes.

But whether the other decorations were plain or simple, the homes modest or affluent, the lighted candles that "gleamed like tiny stars from every bough and shed a soft radiance that bathed the whole scene in loveliness" were the crowning glory of all Christmas trees.

During the next few years, from 1861 until around 1870, just when Christmas trees were becoming an integral part of joyful, festive, colorful Southern Christmases, the Civil War changed everything.

Oh, Southerners continued their Christmas celebrations. Over and over in the now-sepia pages of diaries and letters written during

the war years you'll read, "The Yankees couldn't keep Santa away." And you'll read about Christmas celebrations, even parties and festivities that continued in those areas of the South left battle-free. (Many sections of the South were not invaded by the Union troops during those years even though the entire South was economically and humanly affected by the war.)

Yet in all my reading and travel, I found it fascinating that there was never any mention of the Christmas tree as a major symbol or part of the Christmas celebration during those wartime holidays.

Of course Christmas trees were known before the war; we've proof of that. Yet this absence of their mention suggests to me that Christmas trees must not have been such a widespread and important part of everyone's

The eighteenth-century firebucket, never out of reach, we hope won't provide the flood for Noah's Ark, a favorite mid-nineteenth-century Christmas toy. Imagine a child's fun on Christmas morning when he or she removed the roof from the ark to find it filled with animals, two-by-two. Georgia Room, Winterthur Museum, Winterthur, Delaware

Christmas in the South—the way Santa and gifts and other traditions were—until the 1870s and 1880s.

Clearly, it was during the last quarter of the nineteenth century that the Christmas tree became a time-honored tradition in Southern Christmases. But how much beauty and delight the Christmas tree has brought into our lives since then!

By the close of the century, large floor-to-ceiling Christmas trees became popular in Southern parlors and front rooms. At the same time, smaller trees placed in individual rooms throughout the house were also holiday traditions. And for those who think "theme" trees are a twentieth-century fashion, know that many nineteenth-century trees were decorated in one motif. Tussie-mussies, those charming bouquets of flowers that have once again captured our imagination, were often used to decorate nineteenth-century trees, as were flags and banners and religious motifs.

Furthermore, many quaint, now-antique Christmas decorations that we dearly love today first became available through stores and catalogues in the 1870s. Before that time, simple cardboard and paper figures cut out and trimmed in tinsel were made at home. By the end of the nineteenth century, delicate blown-glass balls, intricately detailed silver- or gold-faced embossed cardboard figures called "Dresdens," and fanciful tin and wax ornaments were bought—one or two at a time—and carefully saved from year to year. And by the twentieth century, special trips to buy Christmas decorations were just as much a part of the pre-Christmas activities as the trips to buy presents.

Today, Southern Christmas trees continue to charm everyone with their infinite variety. Some are glorious religious trees like the white and gold Chrismon tree begun in the Ascension Lutheran Church in Danville, Virginia. Others are magnificent, oversize fantasy trees like those on every corner at Walt Disney World in Orlando, Florida. Then there are the most special trees of all—those in our own homes.

Every family has its own Christmas traditions. Yet over the years the Christmas tree has become the universal symbol that brings the past into the present. And how lovely the past and present can be side by side.

Gracing the boughs of our family trees, quaint ornaments that spark tender childhood recollections cuddle next to those we bought just last year or the year before. A grandmother's or great-grandmother's delicate glass-bead garland gracefully loops around sturdy, durable wooden figures. Each ornament is a star in itself. Yet none is obtrusive; they all blend together beautifully.

Since the mid-nineteenth century, in every Southern home—where there is a Christmas tree—whether a bushy pine from the Georgia woods or a regal fraser fir grown in the North Carolina mountains—you find a living family album, its limbs home to generations of memories at this most loved time of the year.

Handmade golden, crystal, and tapestry ornaments decorate the Williamsburg Inn Christmas tree (top). Above is a tree re-created as it would have been decorated in the 1930s at Bassett Hall, the Rockefellers' Williamsburg home.

Seen from the window of historic Boone Tavern, the Berea College community tree (left) brightens the village square. Berea, Kentucky

A diminutive feather tree hung with just a few glass ornaments (opposite) adds a touch of festivity to other cherished objects—a lace and embroidered neckpiece, a hair jewelry brooch, a demitasse cup and saucer commemorating Queen Victoria's Diamond Jubilee in 1897, and a bisque figurine given as an advertising piece by a local coffee and tea specialty shop in the early 1900s. Hunter House Museum, Norfolk, Virginia

Can I forget those stockings, filled
From top to bulging toe
By mother hands, at Christmas-time,
Within the long ago?
  "My Christmas Day,"
  Helen D'Aubry Durana

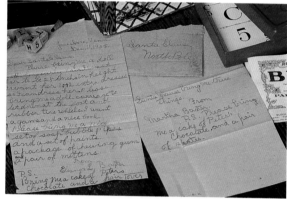

Santa and Christmas Gifts

"NEVER-TO-BE-FORGOTTEN GIFTS"

Those who say Christmas presents are only "things" and mean nothing to them have never closed their eyes and remembered Christmases past. Truly, if Christmas presents are only things, then the spirit of giving—and receiving— has been lost.

One night on our trip after a long day of travel, research, and photographing, when I got back to my hotel room, there, next to the chocolate mint laid out as a goodnight treat, was a sweet dreams message: "We tire of those pleasures we take, but never of those we give."

83

No story captures the true spirit of Christmas gifts better than "The Gift of the Magi" by O. Henry—the tale of the young couple who sacrificed each one's greatest treasure for the other. In Greensboro, North Carolina, O. Henry's birthplace, the Historical Society decorates a commemorative tree with objects from his stories. Here we see Jim's watch and Stella's comb.

The sentiment is endearing throughout the year. Yet how particularly appropriate it seemed to me that December night when I was temporarily away from my home and family. At no other time do we give more pleasure, and feel more rewarded for our efforts, than at Christmas, when we glimpse the smiles and the delight our tangible gifts have brought.

I must have been about seven. It was still dark that Christmas morning when my heart leapt up, but I carefully and silently crept out of bed. Instinctively I knew no one else was as eager for the morning to dawn as I was, so I slipped from between the warm bedcovers ever so quietly. I can still remember how icy cold the pine floor felt to my bare feet as I tiptoed from my room into the hallway. (Those were the days before wall-to-wall carpeting.)

In little ballerina steps I edged my way past my parents' room to the balustrade around the upstairs hall. That Christmas morning my object was to slip downstairs without making a single floor-squeaking step that would awaken Mother and Daddy.

I can still feel the sturdy, round banister posts between my child's fingers as I half-crawled, half-floated down the steps toward the Christmas tree my parents had finished decorating only a few hours earlier. I can still remember the quiet hush of the house. But most of all I remember the first breathtaking sight of the Christmas tree.

There, among the shimmering silver icicles and colorful glass balls, on a tiny coat hanger, hung a blue coat with smocking around the yoke. A few branches away was a matching dress. If the coat and dress were there, the beautiful big-eyed doll of my dreams had to be there, too. She was. And so was the fluffiest, softest, white toy kitten I had ever seen in my whole life.

I was so thrilled I squealed out loud! I didn't know which to do first—run to wake up my parents or to hug the kitty. In that moment of pause, Mother and Daddy called out "Merry Christmas!" They had been downstairs all along. How could they have missed seeing the indescribable ecstasy on their child's face that Christmas morning?

Years later, the summer before I went off to college, I carefully packed my by-then one-eared and tailless but still adored kitten in the red striped hatbox among other precious childhood memories for safekeeping. When I told Mother what I had done she said how she really couldn't afford the doll and her clothes, and the kitty that Christmas. Yet somehow the money had been found. I turned my teenage-deaf ear then, but later as I Santa-shopped for my own small children I often recalled her words and managed to stretch my dollars.

Today our children are grown and we, like families everywhere, have gone through the same process of packing toys away when distant colleges beckoned Langdon and Joslin. The Lego blocks and G.I. Joes, Tonka trucks and Mr. Cucumber, were boxed up first. Two years later, carefully labeled boxes of dollhouse furniture and well-worn, mismatched teaset pieces were carted up the attic steps. Now, each December when I climb the steps to retrieve our collection of Christmas decorations those same brown cardboard boxes never fail to catch my eye. For our family these cartons hold years of precious memories, hours of childhood play, little sacrifices, and loving thoughts.

Throughout the South, generations of a family's things are lovingly brought out of storage each Christmastime as Southerners celebrate their traditions and heritage.

That's what I found in a charming borough close to the North Carolina-Tennessee line. On the December night we arrived at Jonesborough, Tennessee, I stepped back in time. There, just unpacked from trunks and boxes, among

Even cold December days must have been cheery when Martha and Eleanor Baxter served tea to their dolls (right). Their letters to Santa (above right) are little different from those written almost a hundred years later. Naff-Baxter-Henley House, Jonesborough, Tennessee

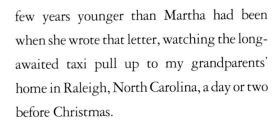

Gifts and toys and antique trunks just seem to go together naturally (above and below).
∾

fragile laces and demitasse cups, heirloom silver and family photograph albums, were letters written to Santa by two little sisters, Martha and Eleanor Baxter, at the turn of the century.

Reading Martha's letter written on December 6, 1905, that asked for a big doll and one or two dresses extra "so I can dress her when I want to," I paused and wondered what had happened to my letter to Santa Claus that memorable year I received the doll, her clothes, *and* the kitten.

"Please bring me a nice book and a game of cards," I read on through the letters. A little doll cradle, some skates, a pair of mittens and a set of furs, chewing gum...the sisters requested in their large, schoolgirl handwriting. One year Martha wanted a ring so badly she underlined it. That was the year she also asked for a toy automobile and a horn or two. Can't you see the tomboy and the young lady struggling in the same little body!

Looking out of the window of the Baxter home, warm and snug on that sleepy Southern street, I was transported back to my own childhood. In my mind's eye I saw myself once again, a

few years younger than Martha had been when she wrote that letter, watching the long-awaited taxi pull up to my grandparents' home in Raleigh, North Carolina, a day or two before Christmas.

Everyone in my mother's family gathered there for Christmas, but Aunt Mary had to travel all the way from New York! I watched through the living room window as Aunt Mary, chicly dressed despite her modest music teacher's pay, gathered her suitcase and shopping bag filled with gaily wrapped mystery gifts and made her way to the front door.

In my adoring eyes Aunt Mary was the most beautiful and best-dressed woman in the world. Her naturally wavy hair fell across her shoulder in the glamorous 1940s movie-star look. Her wool Scotch-plaid skirt and matching dark green pullover sweater came from Lord & Taylor. How I wanted a big-girl skirt like hers—one with a real waistband and without those straps that fitted over your shoulder and crossed behind your back to keep the skirt from falling down.

"Aunt Mary! Take off your sweater and skirt and let me put them on," I begged her the moment the hugs and kisses ceased.

My aunt surely winked at Mother as she indulgently took off her skirt and sweater for me to play dress-up in, for that Christmas my gift was a bright red and green plaid skirt she had found at Macy's. Though the white blouse with Peter Pan collar and tucked front, and the cardigan sweater that completed my outfit, were a far cry from Aunt Mary's glamorous

pullover sweater, I've never felt as grown up as I did that Christmas in my skirt with no straps.

Ah, that was so many, many years ago. These days everyone travels to my house. Some years when there's too much to do, I admit I rush through my own gift buying, but I never hurry when looking for my gift to give to Aunt Mary. And though undoubtedly it is a holdover from those skirt-and-sweater days, usually I look for something special that she can wear.

But what could it be this year? I worried as we zigzagged from state to state, trying to get to as many places as possible on our Southern Christmas adventure.

Then in a tiny antiques shop in the French Quarter in New Orleans I found a lovely antique enameled lyre pin set with small robin's-egg blue turquoise stones. What could be more appropriate for Aunt Mary, who spent her life bringing the joy of music to others, than this jeweled musical instrument of old? It was as if this special pin were patiently waiting for me.

Aunt Mary loved her gift. And how it pleases me to see the lyre pinned on her still-stylish outfits. My aunt who taught me so much about beautiful clothes and beautiful music wears her pin often. Glancing at it, I sometimes wonder, Who else might have worn that pin? Might it have been a Christmas present some hundred-plus years ago? Whose hands crafted it once upon a time?

To some that pin is no more than a material possession. To me it is an object of beauty—a personal symbol of all Aunt Mary has meant to me over the years, as well as a silent

voice that speaks of a bygone age. Such gifts are timeless; they link the humanity of one generation to the next. And eventually I hope my daughter or even my granddaughter will take great pleasure in wearing the little lyre pin, bought as a very special Christmas present in New Orleans for my beloved aunt.

Those feelings are deep and quiet. But there's also all the fun, the merriment and

laughter, that come each year when presents appear under our trees or on our doorsteps.

Like the package that arrives by UPS that is so big our deliveryman has to stretch his arms to their full length just to get a grip on the sides of it. Thank goodness the door is wide; otherwise we'd have to open the package outside. The first year I couldn't imagine what was inside; these days we no longer have to guess. I

Gift giving is much more fun when it lasts throughout the day. Between courses at Christmas dinner at New Orleans' Ponchatrain Hotel, William and Sarah opened their presents from Joslin.

☙

just emit a moan and exclaim, my mouth already watering in anticipation, "What is Rosemarie George trying to do? Turn me into a chocolate blimp?" as I dig through the Styrofoam peanuts to get to the good part.

Inside the package, gold-wrapped boxes come in a variety of sizes, from big to huge. Inside each one of these are the most delicious chocolate candies imaginable. If I were to eat one or two pieces a day, I'd still have an ample supply of chocolates on hand at Easter.

So I share them. The trick is to get my weight-conscious friends to help devour these goodies. It's awfully easy to push away a candy box and say, "I can't face another sweet thing."

But who can resist taking a morsel from a silver basket that has a sprig of holly and red ribbon tied to the handle, especially when your hostess exclaims, "My dear friend in Akron sent these to me and I want to share them with you!"

That's what my guests hear each time I pass the succulent chocolates around. What they do not hear are my secret thoughts of how I wish I could see my friend, her daughter Kathleen, and the new grandson. What they do not see are my memories of always-smiling, effervescent Rosemarie.

To me, those who say thoughtful Christmas presents are only "things" have missed the joy of association that comes when things— whether costly or homemade, beautiful or simple, full of sentiment or just for fun— remind us of those friends and family who live in our hearts year-round.

At Green Leaves in Natchez, stockings were hung on chairs and sofas—and they still are today. Long ago, the children could only peep into the parlor as they were paraded from their bedrooms to the kitchen. They had to eat breakfast before having their "Christmas." This assortment of toys and angels spans three generations in this house that has been in the same family since 1849. Virginia Morrison, Natchez, Mississippi

"LOVE THE GIVER"

~

If memories are the soul of the past, mementos are the heart. And at no time of the year is my heart—or my home—more overflowing than at Christmas.

One whiff of freshly cut evergreen bough or even a glimpse of a single snowflake is enough to send me scurrying to unpack the Christmas decorations. I know I'm rushing the season, but each year I look forward to remembering ornaments old and new and discovering that inevitable small, forgotten something I neglected the year before. Last winter, though, as I pulled a few boxes out of the closet and was getting ready to open the first one, I noticed a large, square package I had no recollection of at all. Why this was almost as exciting as a Christmas present!

Opening a first bundle wrapped in white tissue paper, I found, rather than an ornament, a miniature Victorian flower vase, no more than an inch-and-a-half tall, yet large enough for someone to have painted a bouquet of rosebuds on it. Next I discovered a doll's tea set with four cups so tiny they couldn't possibly hold more than a single drop of tea each. How could I have put these wonderful things away—and put them from my mind, I wondered.

Slowly the memory returned. When we were moving several years ago, I had painstakingly packed away what had been my grandmothers' and even great-grandmothers' dearest

possessions. Somehow this box had been overlooked, gotten tucked back in the closet, and eventually mixed in with the Christmas decorations. I carefully unwrapped the next unknown treasure.

I held a fragile cup in my hand. Its handle had been broken off years ago. Its worn, golden lip was now cracked in two places. But on the front, still clearly visible, was a border of feathery gold, green, and pink petals encircling the words *Love the giver*. Such an endearing phrase, I mused as I laid the cup to one side and anxiously turned my attention to the more familiar cache of Christmas ornaments.

Ah, there were the four porcelain choirboys and -girls I had given my mother for Christmas in 1953, the year I sang "O Holy Night" at our church pageant, quivering the entire time. How perfect those china figurines seemed to me then. They didn't sing off pitch. They were never nervous, and they never forgot the words. Twenty-two years later Mother gave the figures back to me as a special gift the year my own children wore white vestments and black choir robes and sang like angels in the Christmas Eve choir. One day I will give two of the figures to each of my two children when their own children sing in a Christmas pageant—whenever that may be.

Next, I unwrapped thirty-two starched, white, hand-crocheted snowflake ornaments made by my husband's aunt. For twenty-five years their intricate, lacy designs have graced our stately fir. How many nights, I wondered, did it take for her to weave their magic?

The cup is cracked, but its sentiment will endure forever. Around it are the objects I have loved and have delighted in giving to those I love.

~

I always know what is in the long, flat box even before I open it—our own children's youthful attempts to paint balsamwood Christmas decorations. Little Jack Horner's red jacket has one green sleeve. Jill, always blond in the storybooks, has dark, brown hair—the same color as my little girl's hair. And poor Little Miss Muffet. She never did get completely painted that year or any year since.

In the box I always save for last is a kissing ring my father and I made in 1948 by tying two wooden needlework hoops together and painting them gold. In the center we glued two rosy-cheeked cherubs in flowing gowns, their heart-shaped lips never to be parted. Mother always hung it in the front hall and there, during my teen-age years, my sweetest holiday kisses were stolen, with her approval. Each year I decorate it with a sprig of mistletoe, just as she did.

Surrounded by my own dearest possessions brought out of safekeeping for the happiest and most sentimental family season, Christmas, my thoughts somehow returned to that dear, cracked cup. Holding it once again, I reread its faded message, "Love the giver."

Glancing up, my eyes fell upon the choirboys, the balsam-wood figures, the kissing ring. Only this time I saw more than the objects. I saw my mother in her youth, my children, faces and fingers smudged with paint, my father in his workshop.

At that moment I suddenly realized that I cherish these mementos so much, not for their own sake, but because I love the giver. If only I could give back some of that love, I thought.

Then it came to me.

I left the Christmas ornaments where they were that night. Instead of beginning to set them about, I spent my hours gathering together objects I loved throughout the house to give to those I love.

For Joslin I chose a pair of gold earrings with small pearls around a deep blue turquoise center stone given to me by her grandparents the Christmas after I was married. I seldom wear them now. She should enjoy them while she is young, not later.

For Langdon I chose a Saint Christopher's medal given to me in high school by my sweetheart who long ago traveled far away to see new lands and learn about life.

For my then ten-year-old twin nephews, Mac and Camp, and twelve-year-old niece, Tillie, I wrapped up Hardy Boys and Nancy Drew books I had read when I was their age—wonderful adventure stories that had filled many lonesome childhood hours with escapades and dreams.

For a special friend who collects old silver, I polished a pair of antique spoons she had once admired. Though some people would complain their edges are worn, I know that to her their mellow sheen and satiny finish would reflect years of loving use.

None of the gifts I selected were expensive. I'd probably have spent more money if I had gone shopping. But each was a token of love, and no price tag can be put on gifts from the heart given to those you love. So on each package I hung a simple tag, "Love the giver."

Our family Santa's bag is filled with gifts and mementoes that remind us of years past.
❧

"A GIFT OF WARMTH AND TENDERNESS"

"My boy, learn the pleasure of giving."

Santa Claus's Partner, *Thomas Nelson Page*

*L*ong before Santa dropped down any chimney—his sack filled with curly haired dolls, toy horns, drums, teas sets, and hobby-horses—eighteenth-century servant children in colonial Virginia looked forward to their very special Christmas gifts, for they were among the few receiving Christmas presents in those days. Interestingly, the tradition of giving gifts to the servants and slaves in the colonial South unquestionably was as much a part of Christmas as holly and mistletoe. And the origins were the same.

In medieval England landlords gave gifts of food to their tenants at New Year's. During later centuries, after the feudal system disappeared, English servants and apprentices passed around a "Christmas box" into which were put tips and small gifts from their employers.

Halfway around the world, the promise of a special gift made Christmas morning a long-awaited time for Southern servants and slaves. On December 25, 1773, Philip Fithian wrote in his diary that he gave "half a Bit" to Nelson, the servant boy who made his fire. Some century-and-a-half later, in *A Plantation Christmas*, Julia Peterkin described eighteenth-century

servants slipping "into the Big House on tiptoe so they can catch everyone there with a shouted 'Christmas Gift!' before the kitchen fire is even started or the water put on to boil for the morning coffee."

Over and over, Southern diaries and fiction alike tell how the household staff ran through the house on Christmas morning awakening everyone as they knocked on doors or burst into rooms, all the time shouting, "I catch you," "I see you first," or "I surprise you!" Timid servants hid behind doors or around corners, waiting to jump out to surprise the family members. Regardless of the method, the result was the same—a Christmas "gift."

Gift-giving among family members in America was not widespread in the eighteenth century, though of course there were excep-

Charity baskets for the less fortunate have long been part of Southern Christmases. In New Orleans locally made baskets filled with black-eyed peas or red beans, rice, yams and white potatoes, chayotes (a winter squash), pecans, fruits, dried figs, and spices were packed for maiden aunts, elderly cousins, and needy families as well as the less fortunate. Gallier House, New Orleans, Louisiana

tions, especially among the American gentry. For example, we know that in 1759 George Washington made a list of presents for his stepchildren, five-year-old Jackie and three-year-old Patsy, that included a cuckoo, turnabout parrot, bird on bellows, aviary, and "a neat dress'd Wax Baby."

By the 1840s though, exchanging family gifts had become part of almost everyone's Christmas. Southern newspapers like the *Mississippi Free Trader* were filled with ads that promised shoppers everything from "a full suit to the smallest trinket or present." In Raleigh, North Carolina, jeweler Henry Mahler boasted on December 14, 1853, that he had "just returned from a Northern city, with a rich assortment of articles suitable for Christmas presents."

But what about Santa? While we can't attach an exact date or specific origin to Santa Claus, by the early nineteenth century that traditional, bewhiskered bringer of Christmas gifts was a regular and long-anticipated Christmas visitor to Southern homes.

Historically we know that the early Dutch settlers brought the legend of St. Nicholas, or

On December 24, 1885, the citizens of Sumner, Georgia, "all repaired to the school house in a body to see the handsome Xmas tree, laden with gifts which old Santa Claus...was want to present." Today "old Santa" makes a special visit to keep those century-old customs alive. Georgia Agrirama, Tifton, Georgia

Sinterklaas (pronounce it and you'll hear "Santa Claus"), the fourth- or fifth-century saint whose miracles to the unfortunate made him beloved by all, with them to what is now New York State. Close by, the Germans brought the tradition of the gift-bearing Christ Child, known as *KristKindlein* (which became anglicized into Kriss Kringle) to their Pennsylvania settlements. Just to the south, in the German community of Baltimore, Maryland, the children awaited a Christmas-morning visit from the same Kriss Kringle who visited their Northern neighbors. But far away, in the deep South, New Orleans children awaited a visit from Papa Noël, the French Santa Claus.

Eventually, as early nineteenth-century families traveled and moved from one section of the country to the other taking their old-country traditions with them, all these diverse Santa Clauses melded into one jovial, gift-giving American Christmas spirit. Up to that time, however, Santa had often been depicted as a lean, thin, stern figure who carried both switches and presents in his bag—quite a different image from our "jolly old Saint Nicholas." His transformation (much for the better, we all agree) can be traced to a poem, a picture, and a large dose of our human yearning for goodness and joy, especially at Christmas.

First came Dr. Clement C. Moore's 1822 poem, "Visit from St. Nicholas," which today we simply call "The Night Before Christmas." Then, forty-one years later, Thomas Nast's 1863 heartwarming illustrations of a jovial, puffy-cheeked Santa were published in *Harper's*

Weekly. Moore's words and Nash's pictures were perfectly matched. Who could resist an always laughing, nonjudgmental and ever-forgiving Santa Claus? That is the image that has lived in the hearts of all children and adults everywhere ever since.

Southerners took that jovial Santa Claus so much to heart that soon they spoke of Santa as if he were a kindly uncle or neighbor and nicknamed him "Old Sandy." From privileged white boys in nineteenth-century antebellum North Carolina to Willie and the other black children in Roark Bradford's charming morality play-story "How Come Christmas," written almost a century later, everyone called him "Old Sandy." A Tennessee-born Pulitzer Prize winner, Bradford intertwined the stories of Christ and Santa Claus into a touching story told in black Louisiana dialect that speaks to the child in all of us.

Another Southern legend explains why, when Santa arrives, there are always stockings waiting to be filled. The story says that on the night when rich treasures were being showered upon the Christ Child, the only token one poor shepherd had to offer was a humble gift of stockings. I find this myth to be in the true spirit of Christmas.

By the 1830s stockings were being hung with care on mantels from Maryland to Louisiana. In fact, many new nineteenth-century traditions were beginning to replace eighteenth-century Christmas customs. No longer do we find the joyful shouts of "Christmas gift!" written about. Rather, in entries such as the

SLY SANTA CLAUS

All the house was asleep,
And the fire burning low,
When, from far up the chimney,
Came down a "Ho! ho!"
And a little, round man
With a terrible scratching,
Dropped into the room
With a wink that was catching.
Yes, down he came, bumping,
And thumping, and jumping,
And picking himself up without
*   sign of a bruise!*
"Ho! ho!" he kept on,
As if bursting with cheer.
"Good children, gay children,
Glad children, see here!
I have brought you fine dolls,
And gay trumpets, and rings,
Noah's arks, and bright skates,
And a host of good things!
I have brought a whole sackful,
A packful, a hackful!
Come hither, come hither,
*   come hither and choose!*
Ho! ho! What is this?
Why, they all are asleep!
But their stockings are up,
And my presents will keep!
So, in with the candies,
The books, and the toys;
All the goodies I have
For the good girls and boys.

I'll ram them, and jam them,
And slam them, and cram them;
All the stockings will hold while the
*   tired youngsters snooze."*
All the while his round shoulders
Kept ducking and ducking;
And his little, fat fingers
Kept tucking and tucking;
Until every stocking
Bulged out, on the wall,
As if it were bursting,
And ready to fall.
And then, all at once,
With a whisk and a whistle,
And twisting himself
Like a tough bit of gristle,
He bounced up again,
Like the down of a thistle,
And nothing was left but the prints
*   of his shoes.*

—Mrs. C. S. Stone

SANDY CLAUS AND LITTLE JESUS

*I*n a timeless story by Roark Bradford, when Sandy Claus, himself the father of nine children, heard that Jesus was born he had to take him a gift because "You got to give a new baby somethin', or else you got bad luck." So Claus took a big red apple out of the kitchen. But when he got to Miss Mary's house, "ev'ybody was standin' around givin' de Poor Little Jesus presents. Fine presents. Made outn gold and silver and diamonds and silk, and all like dat....And when dey seed he didn't brang nothin' but a red apple, dey all laughed."

In the story the gift-givers warn Sandy Claus that when Jesus grows up and becomes king, he will surely chop off Sandy's head because that's what all the other kings do in the Bible. They go around chopping off people's heads.

" 'No mind dat,' say Sandy Claus. 'Y'all jest stand back.' And so he went up to de crib and he pushed away a handful er gold and silver and diamonds and stuff, and handed de Poor Little Jesus dat red apple. 'Hyar, son,' he say, 'take dis old apple. See how she shines?' "

Of course Jesus was so thrilled with the apple that God intervened.

" 'Gold and silver have I a heap of. But verily you sho do know how to handle yo'self around de chilluns,' " God tells Sandy and so, according to this legend, the same day Sandy Claus visits the children is "de same day dat de Poor Little Jesus got bawned. 'Cause dat's de way de Lawd runs things. O' cou'se de Lawd knowed hit wa'n't gonter be long before de Poor Little Jesus growed up and got to be a man. And when he done dat, all de grown fo'ks had him so's dey c'd moan they sins away and lay they burdens down on him, and git happy in they hearts. De Lawd made Jesus for de grown fo'ks. But de Lawd know de chilluns got to have some fun, too, so dat's how come hit's Sandy Claus and Christmas and all."

notation found in a young Virginia girl's diary we read of families hanging up stockings for "white and black of all ages."

Even oral histories recorded in the first part of the twentieth century taken down from interviews with blacks who were born into slavery include fond memories of Christmas stockings. In one such account, Harriet Jones told of how her "mistis," Miss Ellen, hung up stockings for Harriet's children as well as her own. The next morning all the servants and children were up "before day," and "de massa, Mr. Johnny, come an' let everybody in ter see what old Santa brung dem."

This custom was apparently widespread and according to Susan Dabney Smede's description of the stockings in her Mississippi plantation, could be varied and quite colorful. "One Christmas everybody hung up a sock or stocking; a long line, on the hall staircase. There were twenty-two of them, white silk stockings, black silk stockings, thread and cotton and woolen socks and stockings. And at the end of the line was, side by side with the old-fashioned home-spun and home-knit sock of the head of the house, the dainty pink sock of the three-weeks-old baby."

Equally charming is the story about how Andrew Jackson's stepnieces and -nephews, accustomed to finding presents in their stockings on Christmas morning "back home" in Tennessee, turned the tables on the old general and filled their uncle's stocking at the White House. When he learned what they had done, the stoic President Jackson burst into tears

because he had never had any Christmas gifts in his own childhood.

But some Southern Christmas mornings were more raucous than touching and I couldn't help laughing when I read how just a few short years later—in the 1840s—some high-spirited North Carolina boys drove their mother to distraction one Christmas morning. "For several years it was thought indispensable to hang up stockings as receptacles for presents," Kemp Plummer Battle recalled, "but because we threw the loaded stockings at one another and finally one fell into the fire, Mother decreed that

waiters [small trays] and plates should be substituted." Little did their mother know her substitute would lead to even more pranks.

William, one of the younger boys in the family, put his waiter on the steps so he could get to it sooner on Christmas morning, Battle recounted many years later. William, it seems, also "had the habit of talking to himself when much interested. After he went to sleep we removed the candy, cakes, and nuts from his waiter and substituted a piece of cold egg-bread and other articles unpleasant to the taste. While it was still dark he crept down the cold stairs.

This baby's first stocking has seen many Christmases since the turn of the century. Hunter House Museum, Norfolk, Virginia
∾

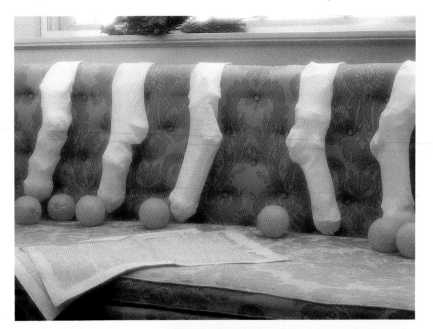

In 1907, Rachel Jackson Lawrence, whose father was the adopted son of Andrew Jackson, recounted how in the early 1800s the children hung their stockings across the back of the big, green sofa "in the General's room" (above). The next morning, they "scampered into my grandfather's room, kissed him as he lay in bed, and wished him a merry Christmas. Then we had our stockings." In those days an orange or two or a bit of lace was considered a bountiful Christmas stocking-stuffer (right). The Hermitage, Nashville, Tennessee

We could hear his words, 'I wonder what Old Sandy has brought me! Here it is! A big slice of cake! I'm going to take a bite!' Then his voice changed to anger. 'Nothing but cold egg-bread! Dog take Old Sandy! I don't want any of

his old egg-bread!' " Reading that account I wondered if the mother secretly wished she had stuck with stockings rather than changing over to waiters and plates!

By the end of the nineteenth century, Christmas stockings no longer had to be one's own socks and stockings. Stores and catalogues offered specially designed, printed Christmas stockings including the "baby's stocking." That was surely inspired by the popular poem "Hang Up the Baby's Stocking" by Emily Huntington Miller:

Hang up the baby's stocking;
Be sure you don't forget;
That dear little dimpled darling!
She ne'er saw Christmas yet;
But I've told her all about it,
And she opened her big blue eyes;
And I'm sure she understood it—
She looked so funny and wise.
Dear! what a tiny stocking!
It doesn't take much to hold
Such little pink toes as baby's
Away from the frost and cold;
But then for the baby's Christmas
It will never do at all!
Why, Santa wouldn't be looking
For anything half so small.
I know what will do for the baby.
I've thought of the very best plan:
I'll borrow a stocking of grandma,
The longest that ever I can;
And you'll hang it by mine, dear mother,
Right here in the corner, so,
And write a letter to Santa,

And fasten it on the toe.
Write, "This is the baby's stocking
That hangs in the corner here;
You never have seen her, Santa,
For she only came this year;
But she's just the blessedest baby!
And now before you go,
Just cram her stocking with goodies,
From the top clean down to the toe."

But babies soon become children, and parents then, just like now, faced another problem: How do you protect those tender little ears from skeptical comments and tricks played on them by older siblings? From North Carolina to Missouri to Georgia, wise parents knew the trick, and around the turn of the century their solution became a charming tradition.

Just before the children went to bed, the father smothered the ashes in the fireplace, telling the children it was necessary so Santa wouldn't get burned. Then after the children were in bed, the adults spread a white sheet on the hearth. Next morning, when the children awakened, the proof of Santa's visit lay in the sooty footprints he had left as he walked from the fireplace to the tree and back.

Mark Twain carried the quaint tradition a step further in his Christmas-morning "Letter from Santa Claus" written to his little daughter, Susie Clemens: "If my boot should leave a stain on the marble, George [the servant] must not holy-stone it away. Leave it there always in memory of my visit; and whenever you look at it or show it to anybody you must let it remind you to be a good little girl."

Similarly, other stories that have passed down in families in literally every Southern state tell how children awakening on Christmas-morning found a smudge of soot on their cheeks, left there by a gentle kiss—some say from Santa, others say from a reindeer.

Once the stockings were emptied and time arrived to open presents, games were often part of the traditional Christmas-morning ritual by the end of the nineteenth century. We know that during the 1850s, presents—toys, books, even pictures and trinket boxes—were often hung among the tree limbs rather than wrapped inside boxes.

Many Southern families added further suspense and anticipation to the fun of Christmas gifts by playing hide-and-seek games. One of the most popular ones was Find the Pickle. Among the manufactured glass Christmas ornaments available by this time was a green pickle. The green tree boughs helped camouflage the pickle, making it hard to find. So when decorating the tree on Christmas Eve, playful parents tried to conceal the pickle among the other decorations. The next morning, at gift-giving time, the sharp-eyed child who found the hidden pickle was rewarded with an extra present.

To play another game, an entire room

The Game of Merry Christmas, an 1898 Parker Brothers game. Juliette Gordon Low Birthplace, Savannah
∾

The elusive ceramic pickle. Smith-McDowell House, Asheville, North Carolina
∾

After seeing this wonderful web of colorful yarn at the Smith-McDowell House in Asheville, North Carolina, Chip and Cindy couldn't resist re-creating the nineteenth-century "spider web" game in their rooms at the Pontchartrain Hotel in New Orleans.

would be turned into a colorfully woven spider-web. Various-colored strings were crisscrossed and intertwined throughout the room to make a maze. Each player (sometimes adults would join in this game) was then given the end of a brightly colored ball of string or yarn. Everyone followed his or her string, weaving in and out, bodies and strings tangling and untangling, until they reached the gift that had been tied to each string somewhere along the way.

Today, should you hear "Christmas hunt," you might immediately envision horses gal-

loping over the frost-kissed bluegrass meadows of Kentucky. But during the early years of the twentieth century, at least one traditional Southern Christmas hunt was as often played indoors as out. The most charming account I found that explained the rules of the game came from my own childhood copy of *The Little Colonel's Christmas Vacation*.

During their pre-Christmas festivities, the Little Colonel and her friends hid little gifts "all ovah the house, from attic to cellah." Later, when close friends or relatives came calling on

Christmas afternoon, the guests chose a card from a Christmas stocking trimmed with holly and tiny sleighbells. Clues written in verse on each card hinted where a gift could be found. For example:

Seek where bygone summers
Have dropped their roses fair.
A little Christmas package
Is waiting for you there.

That particular gift, a little tape measure designed as a ripe cherry with a bee clinging to its side, had been carefully and thoughtfully hidden in an old cloisonné rosejar where a potpourri of rose leaves was kept.

Reading these dear old-fashioned traditions, we may think our own 1990s gift openings have lost a little magic over the years. Perhaps so. Yet how many times have you untied a silver, red, gold, or green ribbon, ripped away the wrapping paper, and opened a box to find a gift so special that you immediately embraced it and knew you had to have more just like it? I know of many collections—some so large they consume bookshelves, tabletops, corner cupboards, even entire rooms—that were begun on Christmas morning.

In our home, Christmas wouldn't be Christmas without the motley collection of stuffed animals jumbled together around the bottom of the tree, or the little houses and cottages that make a village on the den bookcase shelves, or the Beatrix Potter figures who frolic across a table or chest top.

How I enjoyed seeing other people's collections on our trip. In fact, late in the day on

December twenty-third I longed to momentarily cast aside my responsibilities and join the two hundred-plus dolls Frances Parkinson Keyes had collected over the years at the annual dolls' Christmas tea party in her restored home in New Orleans' French Quarter.

As the fading golden rays of the late December afternoon sun streamed through the century-and-a-half-old living room windows, I thought of the place that things both small and large, simple and grand, can have in our spiritual as well as our secular lives.

Suddenly, in my mind's eye I was transported hundreds of miles away to my North Carolina home. Looking around, my eyes fell on my own favorite objects—those things I take for granted but that bring me great pleasure, even comfort, in these too often hurried, busy times.

For the dolls' Christmas tea party, held during Creole Christmas at the Beauregard-Keyes House in New Orleans' French Quarter, miniature invitations are printed and the table is painstakingly set with Blue Willow china.

A WRITER'S INSPIRATION

Not everyone knows Frances Parkinson Keyes's novels, but when I was growing up my mother read every one. At Christmas Mrs. Keyes lovingly wrote vignettes to her dear friends to be shared as "a greeting, a remembrance, a gift of warmth and tenderness, of human faith and generosity."

Today her New Orleans home is open to visitors, who can see the small Madonna and Christmas crèche that she shared in this Christmas poem:

My study is my workshop too
And so my desk provides
Space for the tools I need to do
My writing; but besides,
Among the humdrum working things—
The pencils and the paste,
The pads, the shears, the clips, and
    strings—
Some figurines are placed.
Our Lady's framed by gilded rays
Which give her added glory.
(And when a weary writer prays
It helps to speed a story.)
Nearby a tiny crèche reveals
Our Lord's Nativity

(And when an earnest believer kneels
A Star is there to see.)
The statue came from Canada,
The crèche from Salvador.
(Folk build their shrines both near
    and far
But always to adore.)....
And so through every working day
And every working night
I share the shrine at which I pray,
And find a guiding light.
For Mary and her little Son
A space is always clear—
And thus the Christmas benison
Prevails throughout the year.

The privilege of reading those lines at Frances Parkinson Keyes's desk, in the presence of the personal things that so inspired her, was very special. The moment provided a quiet time to pay personal homage to the pleasure Keyes had given to my mother.

There is the delicate silver basket I keep in the living room and fill with greens in the winter and bright blossoms in the summertime. In my studio hangs a picture of New York, painted in a style that is out of fashion today but was all the rage in 1960. On my dressing table I keep a tiny porcelain box brought to me from England by a friend who died long ago. In the den, high up on a top shelf so it won't get broken, there is the blue and tan pottery pitcher the children chose for me four short years ago. And behind it are books, old and new. Oh, how I love the books! There are so many places and people I have met in books that I would never have known otherwise. There are so many phrases I have read that capture a moment in a way I shall never forget—like Truman Capote's description of a late November Southern morning as "fruitcake weather" in *A Christmas Memory*.

Just as I was putting my thoughts to one side, I heard Chip calling to me. Once again I was in New Orleans. Much work still lay ahead that late December day.

As I picked up my notepad and pen, the sun caught the cornflower blue sapphire in the antique ring my husband had given to me seventeen Christmases ago and that I always wear. Suddenly I realized that each of those objects I had seen in my mind's eye had first come into my life wrapped as Christmas gifts. Christmas just wouldn't be the same without gifts, for when gifts are expressions of love, they are a year-round reminder of the spirit of sharing and friendship.

Santa takes a quick rest at Liberty Hall in Kenansville, North-Carolina (above left). Books (above) were a favorite Christmas gift for Southern children. Hunter House Museum, Norfolk, Virginia

This farmyard toy (left) was given as a Christmas gift in 1856. The family always called it a "Sunday toy." Marilyn Whelpley, Savannah, Georgia

Fireworks and Mummers

Fireworks burst in a riot of color against the quiet sky in Natchitoches, Louisiana. Sizzling-hot yule logs burn at Opryland, Tennessee. Haloed luminaries light the streets of San Antonio, Texas. Cheerful *farolitos* brighten our hearts in Santa Fe, New Mexico. Anvil shootings echo through the valleys of the Appalachian Mountains. Bonfires set on Christmas Eve in Gramercy, Louisiana, billow— while hissing, crackling flames dance in the cressets along the cobblestone and brick streets of Williamsburg, Virginia. Musket firings break the silence of the still December day in Gastonia, North Carolina. If we hadn't traveled far and wide, we would have missed a time-honored, but now mostly forgotten, Southern Christmas tradition—fire and fireworks of all kinds.

"Christmas was really Christmas then," Robert Molloy reminisced about a long-ago Charleston, South Carolina, when sawdust boxes filled to overflowing with big and small cannon crackers, Roman candles, skyrockets and, best of all, scarlet-wrapped bundles of Chinese crackers. Fireworks were as much a part of the nineteenth-century Southern child's Christmas as an orange in the toe of his

At dawn on Christmas Eve, men begin building pyres along the banks of the Mississippi outside of New Orleans. At dusk, the torches are lit and the glow of the bonfires is seen for miles (above and opposite).

stocking. In Short Pump, Virginia, on a back road between Charlottesville and Richmond, "Santa Claus always left a small package of firecrackers in our stockings, and a long Roman candle sticking out the top," wrote Verna Elizabeth Jackson many years ago. The firecrackers were set off immediately, but the Roman candles were saved for evening.

These colorful, noisy, riotous customs

that undoubtedly began with the Yule log during Druid times and eventually grew to include gun shootings and fireworks in England during the Middle Ages, appeared early on in Southern Christmas celebrations, certainly before the arrival of Christmas trees and Santa Claus. Philip Fithian, the plantation tutor whose diary I've referred to, wrote on Christmas Eve, 1773, that "Guns are fired this Evening in the Neighbourhood" and on Christmas Day he awoke to the sound of gunfire all around the house.

Farther South, bonfires, the "shooting in of Christmas," and the Yule log ceremony were part of late-eighteenth-century Georgia Christmas celebrations. The sight must have been quite thrilling as friends gathered at one house where bonfires were lighted for warmth and light. Soon everyone joined in a round of favorite Christmas carols. The children were then sent into the surrounding woods to search for a log that the adults had decorated with magnolia and holly and hidden earlier in the day. When the log was found the Yule log ceremony began.

First a piece of the log was cut off and saved to light the next year's fire. This simple ritual linked year to year down through the ages. Next, oil was sprinkled over the new-found log and three wishes for the upcoming year were made. Using the saved piece from the previous year's log, the fresh Yule log was set afire. A candle lit from the warm fire would then be passed from one person to the next to symbolize Christ's light in the world.

At Winterthur Museum we saw an elaborately dressed mummer, like those in English Yuletide pageants.

or four feet of mud until it was saturated, and then put *this* log at the back of the fire. The mud-soaked log would burn for four, five, or even six days, making the slaves' Christmas last a little longer.

Long after the Yule log ceremonies seem to have quietly disappeared, bonfires remained a part of Southern Christmases. I couldn't help but chuckle when I read in the 1878 Valdosta, Georgia, *Times*: "We can get out on the street, pop six fire-crackers and assemble a larger crowd of boys in five minutes than you will see at church in six months."

From Mississippi to North Carolina, Christmas bonfire celebrations continued in towns and neighborhoods far into the twentieth century, until inevitable fire ordinances snuffed them out. In Raleigh, North Carolina, Tom Alexander recently recalled how, not far from where I now live, the entire neighborhood would assemble and build a huge bonfire of its Christmas trees. This festive annual ritual was the last party of the holiday. Even the inevitable childhood rivalries that are present in every neighborhood were put aside for that not-to-be-missed display, he fondly remembered.

Though we can't have bonfires within the city limits of most towns these days and fireworks are outlawed in many states, Christmas and fireworks historically go together in the South. When I asked my father the main difference he noticed between a Southern and a Northern Christmas in 1937, his first Southern Christmas, he replied in an instant, "Fireworks. We never had them when I was a boy

A century later, during antebellum days, slaves began their own Yule log tradition. Some owners allowed their slaves to "have Christmas" as long as the back log in the fireplace continued to burn. The challenge was to find a green blackgum log, bury it in three

and they were everywhere in the South."

Well, if we're going to put fireworks back into our Southern Christmas traditions we may have to resort to some nineteenth-century tricks. They had some ingenuous ways of making raucous noises back then.

In 1905, Richard Whitaker, recalling his nineteenth-century boyhood in a little book humorously subtitled, *What I Saw and Heard and Thought of People Whom I Knew, and What They Did and Said*, wrote, "From an hour before day until sunrise, the larger boys, who could manage firearms, shot off Christmas guns. We smaller boys made almost as much noise by slamming wide boards upon the frozen ground, and were quite as happy as the big boys." Close by, some other Raleigh children had a quite different type of "Christmas gun."

During the high-spirited days of the annual hog-killing festivities, "Christmas guns" were made for the Mordecai children by the servants who washed and drained the slaughtered pigs' bladders. The children then inflated the bladders by blowing through a quill and hung them up to dry. First thing Christmas morning, the children would take their Christmas guns down and hold them over the fire until they had swelled up fully. They'd then run to their parents' bedroom door, jump on their bulging homemade balloons, exploding them, and cry, "Christmas Gift!"

To be honest, when I read that account of Christmas guns I thought to myself, That custom must have been unique to the Mordecais! You can imagine my surprise when only a

few days later I read in a Mrs. Ellis's Christmas memories that, "Each child as far as they would go, had a bladder, little colored children and all. These bladders were blown up with a reed quill and when inflated to the fullest extent were tied tightly with a string and hung up somewhere till Christmas morning when they were somehow brought in contact with heat, and then such loud reports! I think the 'Bladder Bustin' on Christmas morning was our biggest and most enjoyable thrill."

Whether the bladders were stomped on or popped over the fire, I'm sure you agree that some traditions are better read about than reinstated.

Closely tied to the bonfires and fireworks was "mumming," or masquerading. In recent years mumming, like fireworks, has faded from our Southern Christmas traditions. But during the nineteenth and early years of the twentieth century youthful males, both black and white, considered it a highlight of their Christmas celebration. The mummers were brightly costumed revelers who paraded through the towns, sometimes just noise making, other times performing a burlesquelike skit or play.

The event and the participants were called by many names—mumming, John Connuing (also known as Kooner-johns), Riding the Fantastic, Riding Ragamuffin, and the D.Q.I.s— which is variously said to stand for "Durned Queer Individuals," "Don Quixotes Invincible," and even "Dee-Cue-Eye," supposedly in imitation of the sound made by some of the horns the frolickers blew. And the men and

The Georgia Agrirama reenactment of Riding the Fantastic.
❧

boys' mummers' costumes were equally varied—ranging from clown suits to old ladies' dresses. Though it isn't known exactly where mumming began—some say England, others say Africa and the Caribbean Islands—like so many of our Christmas legends and traditions, the custom interweaves diverse cultures. Regardless, mumming was a very real part of the festive, noisy, and lively spirit of Southern Christmases of an earlier time.

Interestingly, references to this tradition appeared in accounts of earlier Christmases, but were given different names in different places. For example, in North Carolina, the John Kooners are generally known only in the eastern part of the state. Go to Raleigh in the center of the state, and old-timers will tell you about the D.Q.I.s. Head slightly northwest to Cleve-

land County and you'll get an earful about the bygone tradition, Riding Ragamuffin.

Of course, there are many explanations for the dying out over the years of fireworks and masked parades as Christmas traditions. As far back as 1790 a Maryland citizen wrote to the *Maryland Gazette* complaining of "thoughtless boys, giddy lads, or men, promiscuously and precipitately firing through town with firearms, giving their peals of guns when and where they please—night or day." Certainly traditions and cultures change with passing time and we all recognize how different the world is today. But if you happen to be in tiny Rodanthe, located on the Outer Banks of North Carolina, for Old Christmas on January 5, you can enjoy an oyster roast, carol singing, dancing, and the appearance of Old Buck—a cow-hide-and-horn-costumed wooden-frame wild bull maneuvered by a couple of locals. Or if you attend the pre-Christmas festivities at the Georgia Agrirama you can still see the Fantastics ride over dusty country roads on a mid-December afternoon and recapture a quick glimpse of the merry maskers of yesterday.

Black and white children join in for a festive mummers' march in the 1850s with homemade and toy instruments. Roughwood Collection

*In colonial days,
baskets mounted on
tall poles called cressets
were filled with wood
and burned for light
(above left and right).
Colonial Williams-
burg, Virginia*

*"Farolitos (left)
are not luminarias!"
I was told in Santa Fe.
Luminarias date back
to ancient times when
shepherds kept small
fires burning through
the night. Farolitos
are traced to Spanish
traders who adapted
colorful Chinese lan-
terns into festive West-
ernized lanterns used
for decorations.*

109

Drink now the strong beer,
Cut the white loaf here,
The while the meat is a-shredding;
For the rare mince-pie,
And the plums stand by,
To fill the paste that's a-kneading.
"Ceremonies for Christmas"
a seventeenth-century poem
by Robert Herrick

Christmas Dinners, Parties, and Weddings

"LET OVENS BE HOT"

Christmas dinner begins some time in mid-October, when I start thumbing through the November issues of magazines, their pages filled with the latest Thanksgiving and Christmas recipes. How interesting they all sound: crepe ham rollups, almond biscotti, pesto dip, chocolate pepper cookies, Amaretto chocolate cream pie. Filled with enthusiasm, I clip the recipes and resolve to make this year's Christmas dinner a showcase for my rusty, but still-passable culinary skills. Somehow though, as Christmas grows closer, time becomes more precious. There are presents, cards, and decorations still to see about. My

enthusiasm for preparing crepe batter two hours ahead of cooking time suddenly wanes. And the prospect of standing over my three-times-used crepe pan, carefully brushing it lightly with oil when it is just the right temperature, and then drizzling the perfectly chilled batter in a steady stream into the pan—two tiny teaspoons at a time—

In a family cookbook, **Recipes: My Friends' and My Own,** *Mamie McFaddin-Ward's first entry under beverages, "Egg Nogg," calls for 6 fresh eggs, and ½ cup of sugar, 1 pint each of rich cream, milk, and whiskey. To that you add 1 ounce of Jamaica Rum. McFaddin-Ward House, Beaumont, Texas*
∾

begins to sound more like a form of Chinese water torture than a wonderful way to get ready for Christmas dinner.

What's wrong with the same simple but bountiful Christmas meal I have cooked for the past almost-thirty years? I'm much better at decorating the house (it's so easy to put a little boxwood and holly in a bowl) than I am at preparing an elaborate meal. Anyway, how could we possibly call our Christmas meal "Christmas dinner" without the traditional turkey, paper-thin slices of Virginia ham and buttery biscuits, grated sweet potato casserole, and that great delicacy, oyster pie? Which dish

would I omit to make space on the table (and in our stomachs) for the new additions? Each beloved and time-tested family recipe has its own appeal, especially at that indescribable moment when the rich mixture of aromas blend in the kitchen and then creep through the house, making us ravenously hungry. On the first whiff, we conveniently forget that every day of this party-filled holiday season each of us has solemnly vowed never to eat another bite. We shrug off our good intentions and declare that Christmas calories don't count.

Yes, each dish has its own character, its own special way of cooking up just right. There's the way the sweet potato pudding bubbles up around the edges, forming a delicious hard crust around the sides of the baking dish. And what fun it is to watch the succulent juices ooze out of the puffed-up turkey breast as it turns a rich, golden brown, or to see melting golden cheddar cheese spread across the asparagus spears.

Many years ago, I resolved that some things shouldn't be allowed in the microwave oven, and Christmas dinner is one of them. Cooking Christmas dinner should be a slow, leisurely process, a family gathering time, a chance for casual visiting together in the warm, aromatic kitchen—a time for standing and sitting around, sipping a cup of steaming coffee or cider, or perhaps a glass of wine, while the designated cook does his or her own thing. For other families this is a time when everyone pitches in and helps.

Our family falls in that first category.

My kids say it's because I belong to the "Mother, please! I'd rather do it myself" school. I say it's because too many cooks spoil the broth. Anyway, there's only room for so many working bodies in our kitchen at one time. And then, deep down, I always hope that if I do most of the work for the dinner there will be some other eager hands when the inevitable clearing and cleaning up rolls around.

In these days of career women, microwave ovens, and gourmet frozen meals, kitchens don't need to be as large as they once did. Yet every Christmas, when I'm trying to get the turkey and the oyster pie and the dressing *plus* the sweet potato and asparagus casseroles all done at the same time, my oven is never roomy enough to hold all the Christmas dishes.

And what happens to the counter space? I have studied magazine pictures of pristine kitchens showing a turkey on a spotless countertop, or the perfectly peaked whipped cream-topped pumpkin pie, stunning against an uncluttered terra-cotta work surface.

My own kitchen is a mess! It's overflowing with Christmas treats. Why bother to hide the red holly-decorated tin of brownies in the pantry, or the bowl of colorful grapes and kumquats in the refrigerator? They add such a cheerful touch. If I were to put them away, the next person with a craving would simply get them out again.

While I'm mixing and chopping and stirring there is one kitchen visitor who I

could sometimes do without, even though I love him dearly—my cat Scooter. How *does* he recognize the whirl of the eggbeaters whipping up the cream (one of his favorite treats) when he hasn't heard the sound since last year? He manages to jump up onto the counter every time I turn my back. Finally I give in and give him his own spoon to lick.

Otherwise, visitors (no one besides me "stays for the duration") are welcomed as they wander in and out to check on my progress and pitch in to prepare their favorite dish.

Joslin always has to flavor the sweet potato pudding exactly to her liking. The brown sugar, cinnamon, allspice, ginger, cloves, and Karo syrup all have to be perfectly blended and balanced to bring out the flavor of the potatoes. The measurements can't be written down in teaspoons and tablespoons because each year's crop of sweet potatoes is different. Some years they are so

With the sideboard decorated in candles, every other surface in our dining room is covered with the soon-to-be-devoured Christmas dishes.

I've never forgotten the description of the tabletop tree adorned with different colored candles in F. Hopkinson Smith's Colonel Carter's Christmas. *That's why each Christmas I bank the sideboard in a profusion of festive candles.*
⌢

sweet a light dusting of spices and lots of butter is all that is required. Other years when the potatoes are bland and need lots of "doctoring up," we add and add and add, and still ask one another if we've left something out.

Langdon always has to check on the ingredients going into the oyster pie and dressing. That way he can snitch a couple of oysters and, at the same time, be certain no

water chestnuts are added to the dressing.

But everyone joins in toward the end when it's gravy-making time. I can still see my college roommate Susy Booth (now Thurber) explaining to me how to make lumpless gravy. The year was 1958, our freshman year at Mary Washington College in Fredericksburg, Virginia. Susy, a Yankee and one of six children, decided something had to be done with this only-child Southern roommate of hers. Why she thought I needed to know how to make gravy I'll never know, but her "secret" stuck with me and each year I instruct my kids, "You won't have any lumps if you blend equal amounts of flour and fat together before adding any liquid."

We like a hearty, meaty gravy, so while Lang and Joli are stirring the gravy, I chop the gizzards and pull the meat off the turkey neck bone. Scooter always instinctively and inconveniently reappears about that time. The giblet morsels and strings of turkey meat are as tasty to him as they are to us.

Despite the hustle and bustle of these hours, and my own inevitable last-minute panic that everything won't be piping hot or get done at the same moment, this is a time of deep contentment and quiet satisfaction. One of the many wonderful things about Christmas is that each year it gives us a chance to relive our past. I have never said to the children, "Remember the Halloweens when you were seven and nine and twelve and fourteen." Or, "I'll never forget the Fourth of July 1973." But I have some special memory of every Christmas.

Those memories never fail to come flooding back during this most precious dinner preparation time, when we all come together in the kitchen; and they reappear later when our family gathers around the dining room table. The two times are distinctly different.

Dinner, which we eat sometime around four, is a formal occasion in our traditional

A Gift to the Reader
EMYL'S GRATED SWEET POTATO PUDDING

I begin by mixing lots of cloves, allspice, cinnamon sticks, nutmeg and about a cup of water together in a pan to boil on the stove top while I'm peeling and grating. This fills the kitchen with the most wonderful aroma. Who needs those store-bought cannisters of home fragrances or scented candles?

The ingredients below are given in approximate quantities, for this is a recipe that must be doctored up along the way. When the pudding has cooked for about 30 minutes you will have to stir it around to add a little more water, and lick the spoon. At this point decide what extra spices are needed and add them. You may add more Karo syrup or butter as well as spices. Repeat as often as you wish! Generally it takes about an hour and a half for the pudding to bake thoroughly and bubble up to form a sugary-crisp crusty top.

While grating three or four large, bright-orange Jewel sweet potatoes, bring to a slow boil 1/2 teaspoon cinnamon, 1/4 teaspoon (each) ground nutmeg, allspice, ginger, and cloves in 1 cup of water. (Add a stick or two of cinnamon as well for additional cinnamon flavor.) Put the sweet potatoes into a large mixing bowl. Just before removing the pot of spices from the stove, add one stick of butter or margarine, 1/2 cup Karo syrup, 1/2 cup brown sugar and a pinch of salt. Stir while the butter melts. Remove the cinnamon sticks. Pour this mixture over the grated sweet potatoes. Blend well together. Put in a well-buttered casserole dish and place in a preheated 350°F. oven. (At this point I start another cup of water and spices on the stove top, keeping them ready to add as needed, and the whole house Christmasy smelling!)

A Gift to the Reader
OYSTER PIE

You can always tell true Southerners at any breakfast buffet. They're the ones heaping their plates with a crumb-topped, beige concoction. The visitors from elsewhere are the ones timidly asking, "Excuse me, but what is that?" The reply is always the same—"Oyster pie." Oysters, truly a Southern Christmas delicacy, can be served any time. You can toss them into your family dressing recipe, mix up a batch of oyster stew to have with turkey leftovers for supper, or serve them raw on the half-shell. We like oyster pie with our dinner. Nothing is more simple to make—or better—if you like oysters.

¾ cup melted butter	*1 ½ teaspoons salt*
1 cup of bread crumbs broken by hand into pieces about the size of a nickel	*Freshly ground pepper to taste*
	Worcestershire sauce to taste
2 cups coarsely crushed Saltine crackers	*(at least 1 teaspoon)*
½ cup heavy cream	*3 pints oysters, drained*

Melt the butter (real butter truly is best—this is the one time not to be diet or cholesterol conscious) and mix with half of the bread crumbs in a bowl. In a separate bowl, mix the remaining half of the melted butter with the cracker crumbs. Mix the cream, salt, pepper and Worcestershire well in a measuring cup. In a buttered casserole, layer the ingredients, beginning with the oysters topped with a layer of cracker crumbs and bread crumbs. Pour part of the liquid mixture evenly over each layer. Repeat with another layer, ending with a layer of bread crumbs and pour the remaining cream over it all. Bake for 30 minutes in a preheated 400°F. oven. The oysters will remain plump and succulent, but if you wish them well-done, bake a little longer.

Southern dining room. On the sideboard, candles of different colors, sizes, heights, and shapes send out a profusion of twinkling candlelight. I know the etiquette books say it isn't proper to light candles until dusk, but I love both the color and the fairylike glow of candles. Candles symbolically speak to us of the eternal light of Christmas.

The table is set with our finest—plates that must be washed by hand, silver serving dishes I use on special occasions, a beautiful tablecloth and napkins hand-embroidered by hands I've never met, and fragile crystal glasses that I repeatedly tell myself I must not worry about chipping. There really is no reason to have these things of beauty if we do not use them. What good would it be if, many years from now, the children were to get the crystal out of storage in the corner cupboard, or unpack the china hidden in an attic trunk, and wonder what Mother had been keeping "all that stuff" for? I want the children to look back on the Christmases of their youth as a time of festivity and beauty, and carry this tradition with them into their adult lives.

This is why, each and every Christmas, I, like my mother, lovingly take down a pressed-glass bread dish that my father brought south with him from New England in the 1930s. It is quite simple, unlike some of the more elaborate repoussé and heavily chased silver pieces I also enjoy using. The plate was made sometime in the 1870s or 1880s. Though it has been used over and

Traditions reign at our Christmas table, from family silver to pyramids of fruit adapted from the eighteenth-century style. But along the center of the table is a colorful Japanese obi purchased in, of all places, Santa Fe, New Mexico. Today old meets new, East meets West, and each family begins its special Christmas traditions in its own way.

over, there isn't a chip on it. Holding the plate up to the light, I can see imperfections that have been there since the craftsman hand-mixed and poured the molten glass into the mold.

Those little flaws recall a time, now largely lost, when a craftsman took the time and care to make the objects families used in their daily lives. Today almost everything is "stamped out," and each assembly-line piece is no different from the one that came before it or the one that will come after it. But not that plate, nor the sentiment that is expressed around its border: "It is pleasant to labor for those we love." It is also just the

right shape for the mound of ham biscuits I know will soon be devoured. Just think, if I had attempted the crepe ham rollups we might not have taken down that most-special family treasure!

On any Christmas I can glance around the table and see the same pieces—my New England ancestors' plate, the sterling silver nut spoon with the holly motif handle I bought for no other reason than "because it is so Christmasy," my Southern grandparents' water pitcher given to me by Aunt Mary for Christmas 1986—our first Christmas at Saint Mary's. They are vestiges of past family Christmases. Many years from now,

No sentiment is dearer than the one on this plate which we use each Christmas (right).

❧

Fruitcake, ambrosia, pound cake, Southern pecan pie, sinfully rich chocolate cake, fruit-shaped ice creams, and a strong port grace our dessert table (below). Or if you've no room left after dinner, a few kumquats will hold you over until later.

❧

when these same objects have gone to the children's homes for their families' Christmas dinners, they will evoke memories of the Christmases we are living now.

Later, in the quiet of the day as winter's sunlight casts fading shadows through the den window, Clauston and I talk over the day as we take turns trying to keep the fire in the fireplace aglow just a little longer. By now the kids have gone off with their friends, the way they used to go off to play with their Santa-brought toys. They've had enough family time.

I used to do the same thing. So did you. But later in the night they'll be back to make turkey sandwiches, pick at the leftover dressing, and ask, "Who ate the last piece of pecan pie? Can you make one more before we go back to school?"

It is indeed pleasant to labor for those you love.

"'TIS FIT THAT WE SHOULD FEAST AND SING"

From the earliest times, scrumptious food, festive parties, fashionable weddings, and Southern Christmases have been synonymous. Those very same conditions that brought Southern families together for Christmas in the first place—passable roads and leisure time spent away from the fields—also made it possible to have wonderful parties and memorable weddings. Over the years, a constant round of parties—from formal dinners, elegant Christmas teas and festive dances, to informal progressive dinners, even coming-out parties—became an integral part of Southern Christmases. Celebrating these festivities in a joyful, sometimes elegant, sometimes frivolous, fashion seems to have come naturally to gregarious, convivial, fun-loving Southerners.

Christmas spirits in colonial Virginia were so high that a 1746 English publication reported, "All over the Colony, an universal Hospitality reigns." In Williamsburg, the 1765 *Virginia Almanack,* evoking feelings of good cheer, caught the flavor of the season and invited all to enjoy good fellowship in this celebratory verse:

> *Christmas is come, hang on the Pot,*
> *Let Spits turn round and Ovens be hot*
> *Beef, Pork, and Poultry now provide*

A Gift to the Reader
THE NOT-SO-SECRET SMITHFIELD HAM RECIPE

A fully flavored, salty country ham has a taste unlike any Northern honey-baked ham. In the South this recipe has long been "secretly" passed from kitchen to kitchen. The preparation and cooking are simple, but time-consuming. The hard part comes in slicing the thoroughly cooled and set ham paper thin. I take mine around to my butcher, who understands that there are some family traditions that need some outside help.

Scrub and soak a whole Smithfield, or your favorite brand of country ham, overnight, totally submersed in a large tub of water. (I use a large roaster.) Remove and put the ham on a rack in a roasting pan. Add 7 cups of hot liquid. (Water, cider, tea, beer, wine, or water, or as one friend said, "whathaveyou.") Cover loosely with foil. Put into a preheated 500° F. oven. Cook at this temperature for 20 minutes.

Turn oven off. Do not open the oven door. Wait 3 hours. Then turn the oven, still set at 500° F., back on. When this temperature is reached, set time for 20 more minutes. Turn the oven off and let the ham "cogitate" overnight. Do not open the oven door. The next day, open the oven, remove the ham, and then skin it and glaze it as desired.

Children were often served at their own table (above) until toasts and scrumptious desserts brought the family's formal Christmas dinner to a jovial end. Decorating with bright ribbon festoons gathered at the chandelier (right) is a tradition mostly forgotten today. Juliette Gordon Low Birthplace, Savannah, Georgia ❧

To feast thy Neighbours at this Tide.
Then wash all down with good Wine
    and Beer
And so with Mirth conclude the Year.

The next year, the *Almanack* Christmas greeting read:

Now Christmas comes, 'tis fit that we
Should feast and sing, and merry be
Keep open House, let Fiddlers play
A Fig for Cold, sing Care away
And may they who thereat repine
On brown Bread and on small Beer dine.

Feasting and merriment were definitely foremost in everyone's minds at Christmastide. Men used the holidays to enjoy winter's pastimes—hunting, games, and conversation and, of course, courting. For women this was a time for indoor domestic duties—cooking, sewing, conversation (they called it gossiping then), and, of course, courting. How better to indulge in these activities than with friends in magnolia- and holly-decorated homes? Dances, plays, weddings, and anniversary celebrations only added to the festivity of the season.

Spacious, open fields were filled with plentiful game— geese, ducks, doves and pigeons, par-

tridges, turkeys and hens, rabbits, even wild boar. The annual animal butchering provided not just beef and ham but also the suet and marrow to make mincemeat pies (mincemeat is made by mincing pure white suet and lean beef, which is then soaked and fermented in spirits for later baking), porridges, and puddings. Along the coast, oysters—that essential dish for a Southern Christmas dinner—abounded.

Throughout the South, cold cellars were stacked high with sweet potatoes, onions, pumpkins, grapes, and apples. A good harvest produced barrels of peanuts, pecans, and walnuts. But best of all were the Christmas citrus fruits.

As early as the Middle Ages, Europeans had brought dried fruits back from the Orient. During the seventeenth and eighteenth centuries the English and northern Europeans imported citrus fruits from Egypt, India, and the Orient. Among the wealthy, orangeries, conservatories, and greenhouses became all the rage, and a fruit-laden dessert table was a work of art.

Following this tradition, wealthy Southern plantation owners imported both the fruit bearing trees

The boar's head, wassail, and dried apples (top to bottom) were all part of a seventeenth-century Christmas feast at the Adam Thoroughgood House in Virginia Beach, Virginia.
~

Sugar cakes are a Christmas tradition at the Love Feast in Old Salem (left), North Carolina.
~

After a morning hunt, quieter evening games were the nineteenth-century gentleman's fare (top). Meanwhile, the ladies tended to their needlework (above). At fashionable parties (opposite), the supper table was reset for the gala dessert course.

∾

had been dried on their stems), persimmons, and quinces as part of the Southern Christmas table decoration.

Today, of course, Southerners use a profusion of fruits to adorn their houses both inside and out—on living room and den mantels, in garlands that drape banisters and frame doorways, heaped high in simple pottery bowls and gracefully cascading over elaborate silver epergnes. And though fruitcakes, ambrosia, cookies, pies, cakes, and even playful figural ice creams are our twentieth-century Christmas desserts, just like their ancestors of two centuries ago Southerners often still use fruit as a Christmas centerpiece.

Thinking about the myriad and amazing changes that have occurred over the centuries in every aspect of our lives—space travel, laser surgery, telecommunications—it really is amazing how many Southern traditions have survived. When Thomas Nelson Page described an antique mahogany table stretched diagonally across the dining room piled high with turkey, roast beef, and ham, and a shining sideboard, gleaming with crystal and delectable desserts, he could have been describing today's Southern Christmas dining room as easily as the nineteenth-century scene he beheld.

We are indeed fortunate that many detailed descriptions of Southern Christmas tables have survived. Often letters told of the food and decorations for that special meal. These documents help us envision the

and ripened fruits from the West Indies. Eventually the stripling citrus trees matured and produced oranges, grapefruits, and kumquats in the tropical climate of the deep South. But before that time, imported limes, lemons, oranges, and occasionally pineapples were added to the native Southern peaches, apples, pears, pomegranates, grapes (preserved during the winter by burying the clusters in wood ashes), raisins (other grapes

A Gift to the Reader
FRUIT PYRAMIDS

*F*ruit pyramids are easy to make and spectacular looking. This one is much easier to make than the ready-made nail and wood variety. To make one pyramid, from a hobby or floral supply shop buy a Styrofoam cone (many sizes are available, but if you use larger fruits, as I do, a 22-inch-height is recommended), a package of 4½-inch-long green wooden picks (each cone uses about 40 picks so you'll have many left over), a package of short, U-shaped wire pins, and a package of sheet moss (again, you'll have plenty left for other decorations). You also need a sharp paring knife, scissors or snippers, sprigs of evergreen (fir and boxwood), sprays of nandina berries (usually 3 or 4 full sprays

per cone), and 2 full, dried hydrangea blossoms (optional), approximately 8 to 10 each fresh (not ripe-for-eating) red apples, green pears (limes will fade into the greenery) and lemons, and 30 to 36 kumquats. Put the evergreens in water while you are preparing the cone.

Cut approximately 2 inches off the top of the cone, giving it a flat surface. Now wrap the Styrofoam cone in a thin covering of green sheet moss and secure it with the U-shaped wire pins where necessary. Only use a few pins because the next step will also hold the moss in place.

Beginning at the base, put the first pick into the Styrofoam cone at a 45° angle. Moving around the cone, place one pick approximately every 2½ to 3 inches in a staggering fashion so the picks are not in a perfectly straight row. Repeat this procedure every 3½ to 4 inches up (horizontally) the body of the cone. (You should have about 6 "rows.") At the top place a pick straight into the cone. The leftover picks will be used for the kumquats.

Cut the apples in half (across the middle) and the pears lengthwise. Halves are easier to work with than whole fruits. (Leave the lemons whole.) Skewer the fruits onto the picks already in the form, alternating colors, red apples, green pears, yellow lemons. (You may need to make some changes to keep the colors well-mixed.) Stick a plump, shiny apple (a good polishing will bring out the sheen) on top.

Next, put the evergreen sprigs in among the fruits. Pieces with woody stems can be stuck directly into the cone, but use the U-shaped pins to secure these greens if necessary. Let your eye guide you as you now randomly place kumquats you have stuck on green picks into the cone. Add a touch of red where needed by laying small clusters of nandina berries around. These will usually stay in place by themselves, but you may wish to pin them in. Finish the pyramid by adding dabs of the dried hydrangeas. These give a different texture and add contrast to the arrangement.

Pyramids should stay fresh for four or five days; when greens droop or a fruit gets too ripe, replacements can easily be made.

For centuries, inviting, beautiful fruit and food pyramids have been used as table decoratings (above and left).

❧

Tiers of fruits in the eighteenth century pleased the palate as well as the eye. Colonial Williamsburg, Williamsburg, Virginia (above), and Museum of Early Southern Decorative Arts, Winston-Salem, North Carolina (right)
∾

tablescapes of bygone years. Such a letter by Senator William Maclay described the table at President and Mrs. Washington's elegant and formal Virginia Christmas dinner of 1789 as garnished "in the usual tasty way, with images, flowers [artificial]" and filled with apple pies, puddings, iced creams, jellies, watermelons, muskmelons, apples, peaches, and nuts. It was invaluable to the Winterthur curators re-creating Washington's dining room.

Approximately a hundred years later and four states away in Savannah, Georgia, little Daisy Gordon Lawrence had an equally opulent holiday meal. But she tells what no adult would dare mention. Read her charming memories of Christmas dinner as told through a little girl's eyes:

"Christmas Dinner was at two o'clock. The round table which had belonged to my grandfather's father was now extended to a damask-covered oval. A huge flat dish of Granny's prized japonicas was in the center and an array of her best cut glass was at each plate. At this table the grown-ups sat. The children and nurses were at a side table just under the window by the back outside steps to the yard.

"Oyster soup was waiting in the beautiful grape-encrusted silver soup tureen in front of Granny. But before we unfolded our napkins Grandpa said his simple grace. 'For these and all Thy mercies, oh Lord make us truly thankful, through Jesus Christ our Lord, Amen.'

A Gift to the Reader
VIRGINIA POUND CAKE

This recipe (or receipt, as the term came down from Southern mother to daughter until recent years) goes back to my mother's cookbook from the 1930s. Her note in the margin reads, "Billy Margaret {her cousin} thinks it is the best pound cake. It is very simple and never fails."

¾ cup butter	*2 cups flour*
1½ cups sugar	*½ cup sweet milk*
4 eggs	*1 teaspoon vanilla*
1 teaspoon baking powder	

Cream butter and sugar together. Add 3 eggs. Sift baking powder and flour together and add to egg and sugar mixture alternately with milk. Add vanilla. Add the remaining egg. Beat into the batter just a little to mix. Pour mixture into pan and set in refrigerator for 1 hour. Place in cold oven and set temperature at 275°F. Bake for 1 hour. Turn temperature to 300°F. and bake for 40 minutes.

"We were careful not to eat much of the soup. We knew turkey was coming! And when that thirty-pound bird, which had been fattened up for weeks at Grandpa's farm Belmont, near Louisville, Georgia, at last was placed in front of him we could

hardly wait to be served. But this time we came last!

"There was a ham, also from Belmont, already sliced in front of Granny, and then came all the good things that go with such a dinner. Rice (of course), gravy (of course), candied yams (of course), pickled peaches which Peggy and I agreed were nasty, and cauliflower and eggplant—in the same class as pickled peaches!

"And the dessert! For that all of us children were promoted to the big table. A flaming plum pudding replaced the turkey carcass in front of Grandpa and a huge cylinder of homemade ice cream appeared magically in front of Granny. Morrison, Grandpa's butler, and David, hired for the occasion, began making the rounds with napkin-covered bottles. Champagne! Even the children were given a tiny bit, for all must stand and drink the time-honored Toast to Absent Friends. No toast must ever be drunk in water!"

There was one change in the Southern Christmas dinner fare, though. While champagne, cider, toddies, and eggnogs have remained popular Christmas drinks,

Christmas is a season of dinner, parties, and anniversary celebrations. These scenes (top to bottom) represent 18th-, 20th-, and 19th-century Southern table decorations.

beer—so popular in the eighteenth century—is missing from most twentieth-century Southern Christmas dinners.

Even in the mid-nineteenth century, beer was such a natural part of Christmas celebrations that when Mrs. A. J. Ellis wrote "Christmas in Dixie During the War Between the States" for her Johnston Pettigrew Chapter of the United Daughters of the Confederacy, she remarked,

"We must not forget to pay our respects to persimmon beer, a famous Southern beverage. This beer really began back in the summer during the fruit drying time. The good sound apple peelings were nicely dried, sacked up and hung out in the dairy for beer-making just before Christmas. A large water-tight barrel was procured, the bottom lined with straw on which were deposited these apple-peelings, persimmons, baked and mashed sweet potatoes. The barrel was then filled with boiling water and left for a while to ferment. When it had fully 'worked' it was drawn out at a spigot, and no imported French wines could touch the kind Uncle Bob made, 'with a forty foot pole,' as a delicious beverage."

Persimmon beer appears in many mid-nineteenth-century Christmas dinner accounts, including one in frontier Georgia described as a "feast of 'possum [or squirrel] sop and tater, oven pone corn bread, Georgia collards, smoked bacon with a 'streak of lean and a streak of fat,' fresh butter, fritters, buttermilk, ginger cake, apple cider and

[per]simmon beer." Of course beer, a tasty drink with plain hearty food, is out of place with our more refined 1990s Christmas dinner. But there isn't a true born-and-bred Southerner whose mouth doesn't water a little when reading that description—though we admit it is for the collards, frit-

Blood-red anthurium, flown in from Hawaii, drape around the handchased, gold-lined sterling silver tumblers and goblets. McFaddin-Ward House, Beaumont, Texas

129

ters, bacon, and oven pone cornbread rather than for the possum or squirrel.

A reference to a true Southern country Christmas feast intrigued me. Just how did the slaves celebrate Christmas during pre-Civil War days, I wondered. It seems Christmas was as festive a time for black people as it was for whites of all classes because during the period between Christmas Day and New Year's many slaves were "free." During Christmas week, some masters gave their slaves passes to go to nearby cities to spend their Christmas money and visit relatives at other plantations. As Julia Peterkin

poignantly wrote in *A Plantation Christmas*, "Christmas Day is the best day of our year. And Christmas Week is our best week."

Despite this cheery information about the slaves' Christmas holiday (secretly I had feared I would find they had little to celebrate at Christmas), I was cautiously skeptical about the passages in novels dealing with the antebellum South that described the slaves' Christmas tables dressed with damask tablecloths and set with beef and mutton. Reading about the Christmas-night dances to which their masters were invited, I thought, how romantic, how *fictional*. Those

A nineteenth-century Southern eggnog party. Roughwood Collection.

Period decorations re-created in historic homes keep alive the styles of earlier times. George Washington's Christmas table at Mount Vernon was set much like this one (far left) at the du Pont Dining Room in Delaware's Winterthur Museum. Lush decorations were the rule at the McFaddin-Ward House in Beaumont, Texas in the 1910s (left), and the Herman-Grimma House in New Orleans (top) during the first half of the nineteenth century.

opening lines of Irwin Russell's well-known poem, "Christmas Night in the Quarters," sounded so idealized:

When merry Christmas day is done,
And Christmas night is just begun;
While clouds in slow procession drift,
To wish the moon-man 'Christmas gift,'
Yet linger overhead, to know
What causes all the stir below;
At Uncle Johnny Booker's ball
The darkies hold high carnival.
From all the country side they throng,
With laughter, shouts, and scraps of song,
Their whole deportment plainly showing
That to the Frolic they are going.

But when I read narratives of Christmas by former slaves, I was amazed at the similarities between fiction and reality. Their descriptions often included lengthy and colorful accounts of large tables set up in the yard, even parties at the "big house," and dances with fiddlers and banjo players that lasted until dawn.

Among the oral histories given by former slaves, one by Robert Hinton recalled, "We had dances and other socials durin' Christmas times," and Fannie Berry echoed the sentiments of slaves throughout the South when she said, "Slaves live jus' fo' Christmas to come around."

There's no question that Southern Christmases have long been a time for spirited celebrations for everyone. In the 1990s, Southerners seem to delight in their

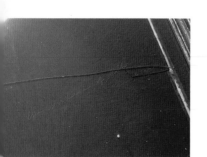

When given a diamond engagement ring, Southern girls were often known to scratch their name and the date into a window pane at their homes, as my husband's great-great grandmother did in Ridge Spring, South Carolina. A long-forgotten poem, "The Window-Panes at Brandon," mentions how this custom was also carried out at Christmas parties held at that grand Tidewater Virginia home. This window is at the Mordecai House in Raleigh, North Carolina.
∾

Christmastime parties more than those given at any other time of year. Yet words sometimes seem inadequate to capture the frivolity, the fervor, the sparkle, the glimmer, the ambience of those pleasurable moments. That's why I found the newspaper account of Mrs. M. F. Harrison's 1878 Christmas night party held at Buffalo Hill, her home a few miles from Louisburg, North Carolina, so endearing. That night some seventy-five friends and neighbors gathered for games, presents, and a dinner that the reporter declared "was one of the most pleasant occasions of the kind which have taken place in these parts in a long while."

Add romance and a wedding to all this happiness and festiveness and the ultimate Christmas spirit and party gaiety become one. As I traveled from state to state, I constantly heard of Southern Christmastime weddings in the various homes we visited. Since my own wedding was on December 29, I felt a special closeness to other Southern brides who married during such a naturally joyful as well as romantic time of year.

At Mt. Vernon I learned that George Washington, who was noted for his love for Christmas, married Martha on January 6, or Twelfth Night, traditionally the last festive day of the season. When admiring the table setting at the Edmondston-Alston House in Charleston, I discovered it was set to commemorate the Edmondstons' fiftieth wedding anniversary of December 25, 1860. At The Hermitage in Tennessee, I heard the

romantic story of how the daughter of one of President Jackson's friends met her future husband at the White House Christmas party in 1831 and was married the next year at the White House.

Much farther down the Mississippi, someone told me how Jefferson Davis, the president of the Confederacy, had met his second wife at a plantation Christmas party. In Savannah, Georgia, when I commented on Juliette Gordon Low's wedding picture, I was told she had married on December 21, 1886, the date of her parents' twenty-ninth wedding anniversary. So it was most appropriate that upstairs in the Low house, now the Girl Scout National Center, in the antique doll house is a bride doll dressed beautifully in her wedding gown.

In fact, Christmas doll weddings were another tradition in the nineteenth-century South. It is little wonder that Mrs. A. J. Ellis and her friends never forgot the wedding she "hosted," when she was about ten or twelve, for her dolls Theodosia Ernest and Johnny Rosemond. Theodosia's dress was in a traditional heirloom style, made from one of her mother's white cross-barred muslin aprons. The groom, however, was most unconven-

tionally dressed. It seems that a friend of the family who visited China had sent elegantly dressed Chinese dolls back home to the children in Morrisville, North Carolina. Unfortunately the dolls had gotten broken and so Mrs. Ellis dressed Johnny in brown brocade silk trousers and a pale blue brocade silk tunic underneath a short navy blue taffeta silk kimono-style jacket, and topped the outfit with a Chinese black serge hat!

Christmas was also the season for slave weddings in the antebellum South. There were accounts of wedding ceremonies—some performed in the "big house" by the master, others in slaves' quarters by a black preacher—and how the bride's mistress would arrange for her slave's trousseau. Many similar diary descriptions, particularly in the deep South, tell of favorite slaves being honored by a wedding in the master's parlor, followed by a wedding meal and cake.

Indeed, the tenderness and loving spirit

Mementos of Juliette Gordon's December 21, 1886, marriage to William Low are displayed at her birthplace in Savannah, Georgia (above). In the children's room a Christmas bride adds a seasonal touch (top).

To keep the season as long as possible, Southern festivities often continue through Twelfth Night. A cake is baked with a pea hidden in one side and a bean in the other. The men are served slices from the side with the bean, the ladies from the side with the pea. The man who finds the bean and the lady who finds the pea become the king and queen of the feast. Chinese Parlor, Winterthur Museum, Winterthur, Delaware
∾

Dessert jellies, fruit juices, citrus, fruits, and preserves made from Virginia cherry, pear, and apple harvests provide a kaleidoscope of Christmas colors among the marzipans, candied walnuts, and flowers on this nineteenth-century glass waiter (opposite). Moses Myers House, Norfolk, Virginia
∾

of the Christmas season traditionally brings out the best in all people. Of all the touching Christmas wedding stories I heard, one told to me by a family friend, George London, was the most endearing. His grandparents had been married at Christmas in the mid-nineteenth century. Every year thereafter on their anniversary they read aloud passages from "Dreamthorp," a sentimental, and rather melancholy, story of bygone Christmases that reminded them then, and us now, of long-ago Christmas romances: "I know that sprig of mistletoe, O Spirit in the midst! Under it I swung the girl I loved—girl no more now than I am a boy—and kissed her [in] spite of blush and pretty shriek."

Passable roads and leisure time out of the fields might have helped bring Southern families and friends together before interstate highways and legalized Christmas holidays, but it is the *loving* spirit of Christmas that really brings us together to celebrate the deeper meaning of the season. When the warm Southern air is full of good cheer and friends are near, we live those words we sing at Christmastime:

Love came down at Christmas
Love all lovely, love divine
Love was born at Christmas:
Stars and angels gave the sign.
Love shall be our token,
Love be yours and love be mine,
Love to God and neighbor,
Love for plea and gift and sign.

The Cock crowed Christum natus est. *(Christ is born.)*

The Raven asked Quando? *(When?)*

The Crow replied Hac nocte. *(This night.)*

The Ox cried out Ubi, ubi? *(Where, where?)*

The Sheep bleated out Bethlehem;

And a voice from Heaven sounded Gloria in Excelsis. *(Glory on High.)*

"Christus Natus Est"

Country Christmases

City dwellers need to take a drive in the country at Christmastime, for on a winter's day, our thoughts become as clear as the crisp, pure air as we make quiet observations of the things that we blindly whiz past at other times. Country Christmases keep us in touch with an earlier time and a simpler life-style that so many of us often forget in our hurried, stress-filled city lives—but that we long to recapture.

What makes wintertime in the country so special? I think it is because when summer's curtain of leaves fall to the ground we see the trees—trees laid

137

The warm December sun will quickly melt the ice coating left the night before on these sweetgum balls. But for now they sparkle like diamonds (above).

Winter's long shadows dot a snow-covered Southern Piedmont field (right).

bare, trees that are strong, resilient to the wind—a resting place for snow, a home for nesting squirrels, a perch for a solitary hawk.

And winter, more than any of the other seasons, reveals nature's art. A tree taken for granted in its spring, summer, and fall dress is transformed into sculpture against the winter sky. Each knotty, twisted limb becomes a line of beauty and the wrinkled coat of its ragged bark speaks to us of time and endurance.

Only in the winter can we peer through the tangle of gnarled limbs into the landscape far beyond. It is there we see a path twisting around a curve before it disappears into the distance and wonder where it leads. On such a day the red tin roof of a house we never noticed before comes clearly into view, and we wonder about the lives of the people who live there.

A country winter day—quite unlike a city winter day—strips away our outer selves, bares our souls, and invites us to take a long, cleansing look at ourselves—to look far into the distance to see where we are going.

When I was a little girl, just after World War II, my family lived on the fringe of the country in North Carolina in a little hamlet that blended town and country lifestyles. During those pre-TV days, that location made us much more "country" than "city." Our neighbors lived much farther away from us than any neighbors I've had since, but I knew every family well—better than I know the people who live around the corner from me now—and their open, expressive faces and earnest, friendly ways left an indelible impression on me.

We had simple Christmases before we moved to a small Virginia city. But my memories of those times are rich.

It was there I heard the legend of how, each year on Christmas Eve, the farm animals would fall down to worship the Christ Child.

138

In my child's heart I believed it for, like the miracle of Bethlehem, the imagery must be embraced, not questioned. And though Shakespeare wrote eloquently of how "the bird of dawning singeth all night long" on Christmas Eve, there is a wonderful, innocent quality to those tales in Southern lore that tell of cocks crowing and bees humming through the long night hours before the break of Christmas morn. Some accounts are brief, like the one by Ellen Mordecai from the 1820s: "The servants used to tell us that rosemary bloomed at Old Christmas and the cattle would all kneel down and say their prayers that night."

Other tellings, like that by Archibald Rutledge, are more descriptive, giving us a stronger feeling of the moment:

"I went one Christmas Eve to the stable yard, and there sat drowsily with my Negro comrade Prince, while the stars blazed, and the pines grieved, and the distant surf roared softly on the sea-island beaches. As midnight approached we became restless, and our nervousness was communicated to the various creatures in the ample old barnyard. The roosters crowed with uncommon vigor and assurance, the hogs grunted with unwonted enthusiasm, and the sheep bleated with strange pathos. After a time, clearly in the moonlight we saw an old ox heave himself for a rise. For a moment he assumed a most singular position; his hind quarters were up, but his head was quite low—he was actually kneeling. Prince pointed him out in awed

triumph. Nor did I raise any question; for deep faith in another human being, even though you may consider it merest superstition, is ever an impressive thing, having about it also a certain sacredness that the

heart with unreflecting wisdom and generosity willingly pays obeisance to.

"Yes, on a plantation, Christmas *falls;* and likewise, every living thing goes down on its knees in the dust before its Maker."

So every year close to Christmas, when Mother would ask "Who will feed the birds?" I never gave it a second thought. It was time to make the birds' Christmas tree. We popped popcorn and strung it. Cranberry garlands were made, not for our indoor tree, but for the birds' outdoor tree. We set little clusters of grapes aside. Suet was wrapped into a ball by winding twine around it. And most fun of all, we spread peanut butter on pinecones. When all was assembled, we tied bright red ribbons around the treats.

Then, walking on fallen leaves that lay

A birds' tree is as rewarding as your indoor tree when cardinal-red and blue jay-blue wings fill evergreen branches with Christmas colors.

Far away across the mountain range there may be a light dusting of snow. But on Grandfather Mountain in the Blue Ridge Mountains of North Carolina, majestic fir trees wear a heavy coat of fresh-fallen snow.

Pinecones dipped in bubbling resin are hung up to dry in the warm Georgia sun (above). Georgia Agrirama, Tifton, Georgia
∾

Mistletoe and holly boughs fill Southern woods with Christmas beauty (right).
∾

on the ground like a winter blanket, hiding the twigs and rocks visible in summer and warming and protecting the plants of spring, we went into the woods behind our country house and decorated the birds' Christmas tree. Our reward would last for days as the dark woods were made brighter by patches of cardinal red and blue jay blue, mixed with sparrow brown and squirrel gray.

While in the woods, we gathered sweetgum and sycamore balls and pinecones to use on our indoor tree. We transformed their prickly, brown forms into shiny, eye-catching decorations by wrapping them in silver foil saved from sticks of chewing gum.

You can imagine my delight, and the memories that came rushing back, when I saw tiers of cones and balls strung in the open window of a log cabin at the Georgia Agrirama in Tifton, a country town in the southwest portion of the state. They were warm copper-brown, and caught the sun-

light like mica. (Today, few people would hang these on their Christmas tree, but if used in wreaths or on mantels and side-boards, they would give a luster to any arrangement.) In Appalachia and throughout the South, children still glue a dab of cotton picked from the summer stalks left in the field to the tips of pinecone scales, bringing a touch of snow inside.

Christmas beauty is everywhere in Southern woods. Winter blooms are most often found in cultivated gardens. But in the woods, clusters of berries—crimson holly, golden pyracantha, waxy-green bayberry, blue cedar, iridescent mistletoe—brighten boughs of shrubs and trees. The somber gray shrub boughs and tree trunks make the gay colors of the berries even brighter. On the

ground brown magnolia cones filled with flat, tear-shaped red seeds lie beneath your steps. In shadowy low areas, patches of feathery green creeping cedar wind their way around rocks and pebbles. Oak trees, their limbs heavy with crisp, golden brown leaves as lovely as crepe-paper garlands, become nature's own Christmas trees.

With so much winter beauty outside, few country people felt the need to bring Christmas indoors—even in the early years of the twentieth century. Oh, some of the larger homes dressed up their entryways and front parlors with garlands of smilax braided with ivy. But winter tasks—making sausage, curing hams over low, slow-burning hickory and applewood timbers, bringing into the barn straw for feed and beds for the

barn animals, chopping the wood, for warmth and cooking, lots of cooking—were time-consuming.

And so by and large, Christmas trees came late to the country. Even today it isn't at all unusual to hear country people tell about seeing their first Christmas tree, not when they were one or two, but when they were older, seven or ten or twelve. Many times their first glimpse of a Christmas tree was a black-and-white picture in the pages of wishbook catalogues sent by the mail-order houses.

There, among pictures of fancy Limoges china, a fringed parasol wicker baby carriage, and little girl tea sets, was a fully decorated Christmas tree with fancy glass balls and embossed gold and silver paper

Even simple country porches are more beautiful when dressed in seasonal greens. Georgia Agrirama, Tifton, Georgia
∾

The simple beauty of country Christmases endures at the Museum of Appalachia in Norris, Tennessee (above). And what better use for a Christmas tree after the season than to transform it into a useful, year-round coat rack (right)?
❧

trumpets and angels. As neighbors passed the catalogues on to friends down the road, the idea of having a Christmas tree spread from house to house.

According to John Rice Irwin at the Museum of Appalachia in Norris, Tennessee, it was just such a picture that around 1910 sent Abigail Ritchie (the mother of Kentucky balladeer Jean Ritchie) into the woods to cut down a Christmas tree for her fourteen children. But rather than an evergreen, she brought home a bare-limbed sourwood and decorated it with apples, popcorn, and ribbons. And so, a special family tradition was born.

By nature, country people are frugal folks, even those who live in two-story frame houses and go into town to shop. So when the Browder estate sale was held in Sweetwater Valley, Tennessee, there among the five-piece Victorian parlor set, Empire chests, and Tiffany "English King" flatware, was a most unusual hat rack. Story has it that each year when the family's Christmas tree was taken down, its limbs were sawed off to different short lengths. The tree was then sanded and finished, and every year one Browder was given his own coat or hat rack!

In the country, Christmas trees often were community events. Grand trees were "grown" at churches, in the town square, in front of the courthouse, or at the schoolhouse or academy. The tree, dressed with gifts for all, was hidden from view by a sheet. Then, when the townspeople had gathered, it was unveiled and Santa distributed the gifts through the crowd. Today we are unfamiliar with the expression "growing the tree." But in the South around the turn of the century, how much fun it must have been to join with friends and neighbors for hymns, carols, a visit from Santa Claus, and the "growing" of the Christmas tree.

One particularly memorable "growing of the tree" occurred on Christmas Eve

Paper chains and popcorn strings made by local mountain school children are no different from those you and I made years ago (above left and above). Simple handicrafts never lose their charm. Museum of Appalachia, Norris, Tennessee

in 1888, when all eyes and hearts were on the beautiful live oak at the Sparks Academy in the Wildgrass section of Georgia, as the area around Tifton was called. And what a happy night it was after a very busy day:

"The day arrived, bright and beautiful, the atmosphere just crisp enough to be

properly tagging the gifts and depositing them upon the Tree. At the conclusion of the work it was found that not a single child and but few grown people in the community had been slighted; besides, there were presents thereon for children and grown persons residing in the LeConte, River Bend, Jewett

In wintertime we see, and delight in, sights we whiz by during other seasons of the year.

pleasant. A beautiful live-oak, selected for the occasion, was hauled to the Academy before breakfast by M. L. Shealy. Mr. J. A. Conaway, assisted by other gentlemen, commenced immediately its erection. By eight o'clock the presents commenced to flow in to the committee, and continued in an almost unbroken stream until nearly nightfall. The committee, with several efficient assistants, were kept quite busy all day receiving and

and other communities. It was, indeed, a grand Tree! As soon as it was dark the Academy was lighted and people commenced to flock thither, and the building was soon filled to overflowing; there was not room enough by half. The giving way of one of the [window] sills, because of the tremendous weight upon it, created a deal of excitement which lasted throughout the entire ceremony of unveiling the Tree and bestowing the gifts." That night the jovial, overflowing crowd of some thousand people was so festive, even Santa Claus, described as having a "hoary head of many winters," was "drown" out. But, the newspaper acclaimed it "withal, a grand success!"

Country people love community gatherings as much today as ever. So in Anson, Texas, people come from all around to Jones County courthouse, almost a hundred years after the first Cowboy's Christmas ball was held, to reenact the event where fiddle music, lovely "wimmin folks," and "the boys" danced until "the dust riz fast an' furious." But even in today's busy world, country people, so festive when together, return to solitary houses at the end of driveways—some no more than short paths bordered by a single shrub on each side, leading from the paved blacktops to the front door. Others stretch so far into the distance that only the worndown tire tracks could lead a stranger to the house at the end.

Inside these houses are simple scenes. These are the homes of many people who still farm and weave and mend and take pride in their crafts. How fortunate we are that these skills have not been lost, but rediscovered and celebrated in recent years.

Today a drive into the country at Christmastime reminds those of us who live in cities of a different era, a time when there were simple presents for the children on Christmas morning—a hobbyhorse made from a tree limb whittled smooth, the horse's

THE ADORATION

Today, living in the city, I still hold dear the spirit of a country Christmas and I recapture it each time I read a simple ballad written around 1950 by the Georgia poet Byron Herbert Reece. Its verses and quiet images are deep and lovely like the woods, generous and unassuming like the woodspeople themselves.

If I but had a little dress,
A little dress of the flax so fair
I'd take it from my clothespress
And give it to Him to wear,
*   To wear,*
And give it to Him to wear.

If I but had a little girdle
A girdle stained with the purple dye,
Or green as grass or green as myrtle
About His waist to tie,
*   To tie,*
About His waist to tie!

If I but had a little coat,
A coat to fit a no-year-old,
I'd button it close about His throat
To cover Him from the cold,
*   The cold,*
To cover Him from the cold.

If I but had a little shoe,
A little shoe as might be found
I'd lace it on with a sheepskin thew
To keep His foot from the ground,
*   The ground,*
To keep His foot from the ground.

If my heart were a shining coin,
A silver coin or a coin of gold
Out of my side I'd it purloin
And give it to Him to hold,
*   To hold,*
And give it to Him to hold.

If my heart were a house also,
A house also with room to spare
I never would suffer my Lord to go
Homeless, but house Him there,
*   O there,*
Homeless, but house Him there!

face a cotton sack stuffed with a mess of straw and grass and its mane a few straggly tufts of yarn; or a rag doll, its wide black eyes and red lips drawn with crayons or stitched with doubled thread. The few storebought toys in backwoods regions might have included a top, a bag of jacks, or a board game.

Crayons, a tuft of wool, and a little stuffing can turn scraps of fabric into a child's dreamed-for Christmas gift (above and below).

Those days if no manufactured games were available, made-up games were plentiful. Nuts gathered in the yards—acorns, hickory nuts, chinquapins, beechnuts—provided all the pieces needed to play Hull Gull or Jack in the Bush, or to make a string of beads for a little girl.

And if the farmhouse yard had a grove

of pecan trees, the ritual of shaking the tree was a holiday event. In *Memory of a Large Christmas*, Lillian Smith recalls how, on tree-shaking day, she and her eight siblings in North Georgia gathered old sheets and spread them beneath the pecan trees:

"We got the baskets without being told. We were gloriously good. Even the little ones listened when Papa told them not to cry if the nuts hit their heads—anyway, they didn't need to get under the tree, did they? Of course, they needed to get under the tree but they said yessuh and waved him goodby as he walked down the tiled walk which led to the street which led to his office.

"The one chosen to shake the tree first was usually the eldest. But now and then, an ambitious underling snatched the honor away by bringing in wood for all twelve fireplaces without being told to or washing and polishing Mother's brougham and offering to drive her out to Cousin Lizzie's....

"Whoever won by fair or foul means the title of shaker of the tree did a pull-up to the first limb, hefted himself to the next, skittered into the branches and began to shake. Thousands of nuts fell until sheets were covered and thickening. Everybody was picking up and filling the baskets, except the little ones who ran round and round, holding their hands up to catch the raining nuts, yelping when hit, dashing to safety, rolling over the big boys' bird dogs, racing back."

And so Christmas in many Southern homes saw scores of pecans stored in pillow sacks, brown paper bags, or large gray crockpots, waiting for the time when the family would gather together to crack them open for later use in cookies and pies.

In our country home the ritual usually took place at night. Armed with nutcrackers and picks, our task would begin. I still have the chrome nutcrackers we used year after year to break each shell so perfectly you could take out the whole nut in one piece, or in two halves if you chose.

A few years ago my citified, New England-born but self-proclaimed "Reconstructed Southern" father picked up a fine, newly acquired, silverplated Tiffany nutcracker from my city-house sideboard drawer. He silently struggled with it until he could contain himself no longer.

"It's pretty. I'm sure it was very expensive. But it doesn't crack a nut worth a damn. Some old-fashioned plain things are just better," he said. Some people would say the same thing about the beauty and simplicity of a Southern country Christmas.

A crackling fire and familiar Christmas melodies are as ageless as the rugged Southern countryside. Museum of Appalachia, Norris, Tennessee
∾

149

*"I'm mighty glad Georgia waited
till after Christmas before it seceded
or it would have ruined the Christmas parties, too."*

Scarlett O'Hara

Civil War Christmases

Many people today wonder what Christmas was really like during the Civil

War years. Needless to say, there was great sorrow throughout the South, as of

course there was in the North. There is a heavy sadness any time loved ones are

apart at this traditional family time. But the fears that accompany war make

wartime Christmases stand apart.

Though I expected to find long, painful accounts of the Christmases of

1861 through 1864, December 25 was seldom noted by more than a line or

two—even in diaries filled with detailed accounts of daily life during the war.

But I did find this moving and eloquent passage written by Catherine Ann

Devereux Edmonston on December 25, 1864, expressing both her personal torment and her larger concerns about the uncertainty of the South's destiny.

"A sad Christmas! In place of Santa Claus bringing me anything—he takes my husband from me for an indefinite time. When will we see a 'Merry' one? 'Merry Christmas,' it seems a mockery thus to salute one in this war torn country. How can we be 'merry' with our best & dearest gone, exposed to Yankee bullets, to danger & to sudden death! We sit quiet spectators of this gigantic game of War, a game where all we hold dear is at stake, when the next turn of the wheel may behold us houseless exiles, wanderers on the face of the Earth!"

Union troops look on as a captured Confederate colonel unwraps his little girl's Christmas doll.
∽

Actually, later memoirs and reminiscences gave more detailed accounts of Civil War Christmases than the letters and diaries written during the war years. But rather than presenting a consistent, uniform Civil War Christmas mood, these clearly showed that conditions varied greatly during that era. Fate, circumstances, and simply where you lived determined life's irreversible course if you were a Southerner during the Civil War years.

Here are two startlingly different memories of a Civil War Christmas. The first paints an unforgettable picture of heroic endurance and struggle. The second tells of life that seems almost normal. Both descriptions, written by Southerners who lived through the Civil War years, provide a deeper understanding of those complex and regrettable times.

∽

We can only imagine the happiness Dr. Haller Nutt believed the future held on Christmas Eve, 1859, when he wrote from Natchez, Mississippi, to Samuel Sloan, a prominent Philadelphia architect, commissioning Sloan to build a gift for his wife, Julia—a grand house totally unlike any other in Natchez. Its tiered and domed exterior would blend the exotic romance of Queen Scheherazade's Arabia with a practical and efficient floor plan that would make today's most energy-conscious designer envious.

To build the six-story structure, both local slaves and skilled workers from Philadelphia were employed. Detailed attention was given to every aspect of the house. Orders were placed for the finest millwork, chandeliers, rosewood cabinets, gilt mirrors—even European statuary.

With the exterior structure completed, the interior work was proceeding on course when the rumbling clouds of war disrupted everything. The bricklayers left to return

A picture and floor plan of a "Villa in the Oriental Style" appeared in the January 1861 Godey's Lady's Book *(above left). Ironically, that villa was Longwood, a Natchez home not completed because the Civil War broke out. Family pictures are reminders of happier times before the Civil War came to Longwood (above).*

north. First, however, they published a notice in the Natchez paper thanking Dr. Nutt "for the very liberal and uniformly kind treatment extended to us during our sojourn with him; and to the citizens of Natchez generally, who have manifested to us the greatest courtesy...."

Though much of the furniture had been delivered (containers in the unfinished portion of the house today remain as they were left well over a century ago), work on the house ceased. The five stories above the basement floor were boarded up and the Nutts and their then seven children lived in the completed basement floor in ever diminishing circumstances.

When the invading Union troops arrived, Yankee-sympathizer Dr. Nutt, who incidentally was a physician, scientist, and progressive planter utilizing highly advanced farming methods, was given "Protection papers" by the Union commanders. Nonetheless, Union troops completely destroyed all "save a few bales of seed cotton and standing corn."

In 1864, shortly before the end of the war, Haller Nutt died of pneumonia and "troubles." Valiant Julia Nutt, now with eight children and two additional dependent families to support, was left penniless. An educated woman of Southern gentry, her own words best tell of her plight:

"I had jewels but I could not sell them. I had dresses but I could not sell them. I had twenty-four cows and while I could keep them I sent my younger son, Prentiss, to Camp every day and sold milk. This supported me and my children but before the year was out the cows were taken from me by U.S. soldiers...."

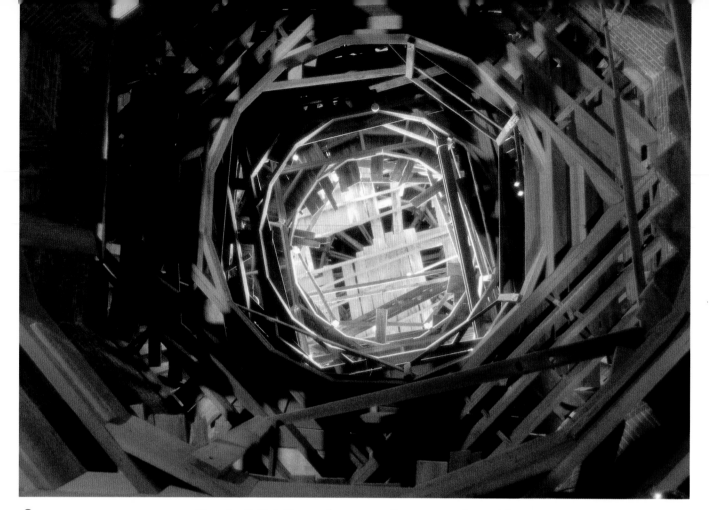

Sturdy timbers erected by Northern laborers and Southern slaves are silent vestiges of Dr. Nutt's unfinished dream—Longwood.
☙

Despite Julia's Protection papers from General Grant, she was stripped of all that could be of any value to the northern troops—her livestock, wagons, harness, even fences and farm tools. But the "last and heaviest blow" came when General Grayman took $8,787 from Dr. Nutt's estate:

"Then came the dark and winter days of my life," she later wrote. "I gathered wild weeds and fed my children on them and when winter came on we thanked God when we could get a little corn. My youngest child was but a baby and my oldest son, just sixteen. How we lived God alone knows."

Though this story is one of heartbreak and devastation, not all the South was so stricken. Of course Christmas in wartime can never be carefree. Yet in other less ravished areas throughout the South, high-spirited Southerners kept the gaiety of the season alive wherever possible.

☙

In the uninvaded North Carolina village of Morrisville, Christmas was made all the more joyful as the neighborhood celebrated "our soldier boys at home on Holiday furloughs." Mrs. A. J. Ellis recalled:

"You just ought to have seen the supper tables. The best white table linen was spread out, cut-glass, silver and 'Sunday' real china, all in place, and the decorations were beautiful to behold. Cedar all powdered white somehow with flour also the hydrangea blooms dried by this time were all powdered white and looked like great white snow-balls. All these white beauties were interspersed with the green holly full of red berries and with frosted cakes, quivering jellies, store candies and glasses of syllabub, all rested among these evergreen and white things when lighted up with candles in silver on highly polished brass candlesticks, defied all description. Back in pantries, or on sideboards or side tables, ready to be passed around were meats—such as hams, chicken, turkey, barbecue, besides custards and cakes of every description were fully enjoyed.... The pretty young ladies in their beautiful home-spun dresses, all made up and trimmed with quantities of buttons covered with contrasting material and other pretty handmade decorations, were so charming that no wonder they 'scorned to wear a bit of silk or a bit of Northern lace.' The young men in spite of the wail of the 'poor ragged Confederate soldiers' managed to be all dressed up in new fresh looking uniforms all resplendent in gold lace and shiney buttons. After supper they danced the old fashion Virginia Reel, Scotch ramble, London Bridge, or played games, such as marching around singing… 'When I lived in the State of Virginia to Carolina I did go, there I saw a handsome lady O, her name I did not know.' Stealing partners and other amusements enlivened the occasion. This is a true picture of Christmas in my neighborhood

during the War Between the States."

I smiled to myself when I read Mrs. Ellis's last sentence. Its frank and almost pleading-to-be-believed tone certainly dispels many of the stories that you and I have heard that only tell of Southern hardships during those four dark years.

The farms and plantations yielded the meats and staples for this grand dinner and, Mrs. Ellis tells us, "sometimes, somehow, the housewives managed to get through the blockade a little sugar and some genuine coffee. So you see it was not so difficult to get up a fine collection of goodies as [it] might be supposed."

Despite this upbeat account of the Civil War years in rural North Carolina, we know that memories of suffering in other parts of the South during this time will live

A rendering of the Confederate capitol in Richmond, Virginia, by Parks Duffey.

in history. But the human spirit is resilient. It is important to seek the light-hearted and the cheerful in such tragic times.

Take the blockade, for instance. On Christmas morning many a Southern Mother blamed the blockade for Santa Claus's absence. Santa couldn't get through the Yankee lines, Southern children were told when the dreamed-for gifts were not there. Other children heard that the Yankees had captured Santa. Yet in later years, many touching stories were told about how Yankee soldiers turned a blind eye as an occasional Confederate risked his life to be home with his wife and children for just a few hours at Christmas.

But what about those Southern soldiers, away from their homes, in the battlefield? Their endurance is legend. The grieving, youthful voice of William McCabe, a Richmond poet, so poignantly captured their painful solitude in "Christmas Night of '62" that the poem was included in popular anthologies over the next fifty years. Here are a few of the lines from the poem that the Confederate veterans held dear.

The wintry blast goes wailing by,
The snow is falling overhead;

. . .

The soldiers cluster round the blaze
To talk of other Christmas days,
And softly speak of home and home.
My thoughts go wandering to and fro,
Vibrating 'twixt the Now and Then;
I see the low-browed home agen,

Crowning the visages of Generals Lee and Jackson, and Jefferson Davis, President of the Confederacy, is a towering Christmas tree (opposite), also reflected in the still pool beneath. Stone Mountain, Georgia

The old hall wreathed with mistletoe.

. . .

My eyes are wet with tender tears.
There's not a comrade here to-night
But knows that loved ones far away
On bended knees this night will pray:
"God bring our daring from the fight."

When the war ended, the return of peace, coupled with the hope of better years ahead was reason to rejoice. Families were reunited. Santa no longer had any blockades to impede his travels. Soon festivity, joy, and splendor would find its way back into Southern Christmases once the "deluge of war" subsided.

What *was* Christmas really like during the Civil War years? It was certainly a time of great sorrow, but it was also a time when hope was found in little things. Like the hope in the little girl's voice when, as others around her are celebrating Christmas, she finds a letter from her father, a prisoner in a Yankee camp:

Old Santa Claus brought heaps of things
To all the other folks;
I heard them Christmas morning say
They are cracking nuts and jokes;
And opening of the packages,
And guessing what they were;
And if this one had come fum him,
And that one camed fum her.
But best of all he brought to me
A letter with a curl;
My papa in the prison wrote,
"God keep my little girl."

Turkey comes table d'hote or a la carte.
Our elevator wears a wreath of holly.
Phyllis McGinley, from "City Christmas"

Christmases Old and New

It couldn't have happened better if I had planned it. We set out from Johnson City, Tennessee, with the rising December sun, drove up to Danville, Kentucky, and then fought the whizzing traffic along I-65 back down to Nashville. The odometer registered some 500-plus miles. All in all, it was one of the longest days we had put in during our tour through fifteen states. Pulling up to the entrance of Opryland, we were as weary as war-tired troops. To be truthful, the children were in better spirits than we adults.

As we turned into the long, winding driveway, William saw the lights first. Five-year-old squeals of delight are indescribable and untranslatable.

Each night at twilight, Opryland, with its sparkling Christmas lights, becomes a fairyland for young and old to behold (above and right). From Nashville to New Orleans (opposite), Southern landcapes are transformed into colorful scenes at Christmastime.

*Christmas cheer
is everywhere at
Opryland.*
∾

Sarah soon joined in, and in no time Nicholas made it a trio. I had a terrible case of laryngitis, otherwise I would have outsquealed them all.

Lights were everywhere. Red, yellow, and green lollipops on peppermint-striped sticks—just like the ones I used to dream about when I was five years old—were so close we could almost touch them. The snow-white icing on the gingerbread-house roof was so real I wanted to run my finger through it for a lick of pure sugar.

In the storybook thrill of the moment, I spontaneously and quite uninhibitedly waved to my new friend, the dancing snowman who welcomed us into a dreamworld of suspended time where childhood fantasies come true. A forest of beautiful Christmas trees lay ahead. Like magic, layers of shimmering, gossamer shapes appeared everyplace we looked. Unexpected splashes of color reflected in deep, still pools twinkled beneath the cobalt blue December

sky. In the far distance we even caught a glimpse of Santa and his reindeer.

Around the bend, Christmas toy soldiers pointed us on our way. We wound through a maze of gumdrop trees and diamond-tipped shrubs until at last, like Hansel and Gretel, we came to our lodging for the night. Ironically, that is where the story really begins.

You and I know that over a million lights can make an exterior more than spectacular. But inside, hotel lobbies are pretty much the same. True enough, other than its large size, the Opryland reception area looked rather like its counterpart in many other grand hotels.

By now it was almost midnight, yet there was much business still to tend to. I dashed to the pay phones, hoping to get in a final call for the day. My disposition, though definitely made more cheerful by the beauty of the outdoor panorama, was nonetheless a little grumpy. Then, as I picked up the phone and fumbled for my credit card with the fourteen-digit code, I overheard the man at the phone next to mine.

"It's wonderful," he was saying, his unmistakable Yankee accent full of smiles. "Just like I remembered it. The people are so friendly. They're all so *Southern*. It's a great place to come back to."

I smiled to myself. My grumpiness quietly melted away.

Early the next morning, I immediately noticed the many three-generation families

who had come from separate starting points for a special Christmas gathering in that heart-warming, festive atmosphere.

Grandfathers pushed babies in strollers. Sociable toddlers, their parents in tow, tottled along the gas-lit walkways. Later that afternoon I saw a remarkable scene. Even usually restless teenagers patiently awaited with their families the daily lighting of the Yule log in the Magnolia Lobby.

Observing these family scenes I thought how, in this modern rush-a-day world, we all need an occasional brush with the fairytale beauty of our childhood. Seeing twinkling lights, returning smiles of holiday cheer from strangers, taking leisurely strolls through lanes that lead us into the picture books of yore, hearing Christmas tunes played on antique music boxes—these are intimate, private times even though they may be spent in the midst of other people.

And, of course, these scenes made me nostalgic. I missed my own family and wished they had been there to share the sights and sounds of Opryland at Christmas. Yet my thoughts were kept warm by memories of Christmas trips our family had taken when the children were young. In fact, several places we visited on this trip had been spots on my family's 1978 Christmas journey to Walt Disney World.

Many wonderful experiences from that trip years ago have remained fresh in our minds and hearts. We drove into Orlando on

In Sante Fe, New Mexico, farolitos are everywhere at Christmastime. They adorn churches, rooftops, humble adobes, walls, ledges, and walkways.

Christmas Eve. The next morning there really wasn't much time for opening presents. Instead, we rushed straight to Walt Disney World to be among the first inside the gates that beautiful, crystal-clear morning. It was well worth the trouble. I can still hear Langdon's words when we first spied Mickey Mouse: "Mickey's our Santa this year!" he chirped.

We each had a "substitute Santa" that day. For Joli, Cinderella was Santa. What little girl wouldn't think Christmas dinner in Cinderella's Castle was a dream come true? For Clauston, Santa's spirit shone in every doll's face in "It's A Small World." To this day he still whistles the lilting tune. Like Wendy, I soared with Peter Pan high above the rooftops of London.

But the most special gift of all was given to us by strangers. Like the man in the telephone booth at Opryland who swept away my grumpiness, I never learned their names. At dusk, in the mellow glow of the setting December sun, as we four walked toward the gates, a gentle-looking older couple approached us.

"Are you coming back tomorrow?" the lady asked.

"Oh yes," we replied in chorus, a little wearily but still enthusiastically.

"One of our grandchildren isn't feeling well and we're going to start home tonight," she explained. "We'd like for you to have the tickets we haven't used."

"Why thank you," Clauston replied, reaching for his wallet. "How many do you have?"

"Oh no," the gentleman protested when he realized Clauston's intention to pay for the tickets. "We can't use them. We want to *give* them to you. Just in the spirit of Christmas," he added matter-of-factly.

The spirit of Christmas doesn't just belong in your own home among your own family. It can be found many miles away in the company of strangers. It can be anyplace where people gather together to enjoy the same pleasures—whether a Christmas wagon ride at Georgia's Agrirama, the lighting of the Yule log at Colonial Williamsburg, Feast Day in Santa Fe, or the Moravian Lovefeast at Old Salem.

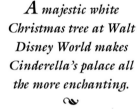

A majestic white Christmas tree at Walt Disney World makes Cinderella's palace all the more enchanting.

Historic Old Salem traces its Christmas history back 225 years when the Moravians settled in the Western Piedmont area of North Carolina. Each year in mid-December, Old Salem becomes a living, breathing nineteenth-century Moravian Christmas card as onlookers come to enjoy life as it was lived there many years ago. Old Salem, Winston-Salem, North Carolina

Traveling back home after seven and a half weeks on the road, I drove into "Christmas Town, U.S.A." This tiny North Carolina textile town celebrates Christmas like no other. As Charles Kuralt said of this little town of McAdenville, of all the towns ablaze with Christmas lights, "none is so small and none is so bright."

∾

Gingerbread houses are favored decorations at resort hotels such as the Williamsburg Inn (right). Nestled at the foot of the Blue Ridge Mountains, the Grove Park Inn in Asheville, North Carolina, has been home to Christmas guests since the 1910s. William (below right) could not stay away from the gingerbread village, complete with electric train. Sarah (below) preferred the model of the Inn itself.

Today, entire cities decked out in Christmas cheer both capture the new and preserve the old. In San Antonio, Texas, streams of twinkling lights dangling above the luminarias light the footbridges and walkways for Las Posadas, the traditional procession that tells how Mary and Joseph were refused room at the inn and sought shelter in the humble stable.

No doorway is left undressed at Christmas in Williamsburg, yet each one is unique and eyecatching. Twentieth-century Williamsburg Christmases wouldn't be complete without colorful fruit decorations adapted from eighteenth-century traditions. The Governor's Palace (above and right) and Colonial Williamsburg residences (opposite).

170

What sweeter music can we bring
Than a carol, for to sing
The birth of this our heavenly King?
Awake the voice! Awake the string....
                    Robert Herrick

The Spirit of Christmas

"When was the last time you stood around the piano and sang?" my friend Lou Johanson asked one balmy April night, her voice full of nostalgia.

"Last Christmas," I replied wistfully, as in my mind's eye the calendar rolled back to a Christmas night that my son, Langdon, and I will remember forever. It was a Christmas night that, though filled with joy, also held the tinge of sadness that can come at a festive time when we know life is slipping by more quickly than we might wish.

Everyone has or has known an "Aunt Mary"—that special woman who, by fate or choice, did not marry but who loves all children and has dedicated her life to their well-being. Your Aunt Mary may be a neighbor, a godmother, your favorite teacher or, like my Aunt Mary, your real aunt. Regardless, you will forever carry her spirit and influence with you in hidden, gentle ways throughout your life.

Our family's Aunt Mary is the family musician. She's the one who harmonizes the alto part when we sing the doxology at Christmas dinner. And over the years she's

Eighteenth-century diaries often tell of the music played and sung at Southern Christmas parties.

the one who always gathered us all together in the living room for the traditional Christmas carol songfest—not just once but every night during the Christmas season.

That was when families stayed in at night, or else all went out together. These days it is hard to catch the entire family together at any time other than mealtime. So over the years our Christmas carol singing time has dwindled to that one time when, after we've had our Christmas dinner, we are Aunt Mary's captive audience, for though

she is now into her mid-eighties and not well, she still plays the piano with the verve and flare of her youth.

But last year, on the day after Christmas, almost by some miracle, circumstances worked out for cousins and aunts and uncles and grandparents from both sides of our family to meet at our house. When putting out the plates for our buffet supper, I stopped counting heads (and mouths) at nineteen, and simply took down an extra stack of mismatched plates. (It's a good thing I did, for in no time a couple of my sister-in-law's stepchildren popped in to see what was going on, and test our leftovers.)

The day was wonderful. All ages were gathered throughout the house—from Heather, my cousin's three-year-old, to my octagenarian aunt. Their various noises and voices reflected the many generations— little-girl giggles, deep masculine laughs, high-pitched squeals drowning out serious adult discussions, the patter of little-boy skipping and running feet.

I was busy in the kitchen when I heard the first sounds of the piano coming from the living room. "There goes Aunt Mary," I smiled to myself, knowing there was no reason to rush getting the food out now.

"It's beginning to look a lot like Christmas," I hummed along to myself, my step lighter, my duties easier.

"Oh little town of Bethlehem." "Jingle bells, jingle bells." "Angels we have heard on high." "Jingle bells, jingle bells." There was no rhyme or reason to the sequence. But what did that matter? All Christmas songs sound great together.

Voices rang out louder and louder as everyone moved into the living room and joined in. But when "Jingle Bells" started anew for the umpteenth time, I decided to peek in myself.

From the hallway, looking through the open door, I could barely see Aunt Mary at the piano. Amanda, her great-grandniece, sat snuggled up next to her on one side. Camp, my nephew on Clauston's side of the family, sat by her other side, his feet dangling off the end of the bench. Everyone was gathered close around the piano, shoulders touching, some holding hands. Young fathers held the little ones up, while my own mother leaned against the end of the grand piano, unconsciously rearranging the bowl of green boughs while she sang. There surely isn't room for me, I thought to myself, when suddenly I realized that Langdon was standing beside me.

"No room for you either?" I laughed.

When he shook his head, no, I saw his tear-filled eyes.

No words were spoken. They weren't needed. They couldn't have said what we both felt in our hearts—what we both saw in our minds.

If Langdon could have had his wish, he would have been a boy again, seated next to Aunt Mary, with his little sister Joli, all bubbly and cheery in her spanking new Christmas-red dress, snuggling close to Aunt Mary's other side.

If I could have had my wish, I would have had Aunt Mary all to myself, the way I did as an only child, in the late 1940s. We both would have frozen time to keep Aunt Mary eternally young, though we, ourselves, would have continued to grow, to live our lives as we chose.

Months later Langdon and I talked about that Christmas-night moment in the hall. There was no embarrassment that we shed a few tears as we remembered the poignancy of the scene. There was no shame.

Rather, we talked about how Christmas rekindles memories that are often too deep for words when we miss times past.

And as best I could, I tried to tell my twenty-one-year-old son that someday, the vision of Aunt Mary, little Amanda and Camp, Granny, and all the other family members singing carols around the piano will bring a grand smile to his lips. Oh, he may have to choke back the tears every so often over the years, but time has a wonderful way of brightening the past so that one day only the smiles will remain.

And so, for Langdon, and for each of you, my Christmas wish is that every time we hear the Christmas carols we love and we sing year after year, that others have sung and will continue to sing century after century, our child's heart will be able to join in joyfully and loudly, as mine did last year, "It's beginning to look a lot like Christmas."

In the early nineteenth century Jews and Gentiles alike came to the Moses-Myer House in Norfolk, Virginia, to celebrate the season with a night of music.
∾

May our child's heart always delight in the joy and mirth of Christmas.

WHY SOUTHERN CHRISTMASES?

∾

We wish you health and good fires; victuals, drink, and good stomachs; innocent diversion, and good company; honest trading, and good success; loving courtship, and good wives; and lastly, a merry CHRISTMAS and a happy New Year.

Virginia Almanack, *1771*

Why Southern Christmases? Perhaps no one has ever said it better, or captured the spirit, heart, and glory of a Christmas day in the South more exquisitely than Henry Woodfin Grady when he wrote, toward the end of the nineteenth century, "A Perfect Christmas Day":

"No man or woman now living will see again such a Christmas day as the one which closed yesterday, when the dying sun piled the western skies with gold and purple.

"A winter day it was, shot to the core with sunshine. It was enchanting to walk abroad in its prodigal beauty, to breathe its elixir, to reach out the hands and plunge them open-fingered through its pulsing waves of warmth and freshness. It was June and November welded and fused into a perfect glory that held the sunshine and snow beneath tender and splendid skies. To have winnowed such a day from the teeming winter was to have found an odorous peach on a bough shipped in the storms of winter.

One caught the musk of yellow grain, the flavor of ripening nuts, the fragrance of strawberries, the exquisite odor of violets, the aroma of all seasoning in the wonderful day. The hum of bees underrode the whistling wings of wild geese flying southward. The fires slept in drowsing grates, while the people, marveling outdoors, watched the soft winds woo the roses and the lilies.

"Truly it was a day of days. Amid its riotous luxury surely life was worth living to hold up the head and breathe it in as thirsting men drink water; to put every sense on its gracious excellence; to throw the hands wide apart and hug whole armsful of the day close to the heart until the heart itself is enraptured and illumined. God's benediction came down with the day, slow dropping from the skies. God's smile was its light, and all through and through its supernal beauty and stillness, unspoken but appealing to every heart and sanctifying every soul, was His invocation and promise, 'Peace on earth, good will to men.'"

Angels on high shout the glad tidings. Saint Mary's College, Raleigh, North Carolina

∾

The voices of Christmas music in the South are lovely and varied. Music, both secular, and sacred, has long brought the spirit of Christmas into our lives and untited different faiths in the hope of eternal peace for all people everywhere—from choirs of angelic voices in the simple wooden chapel at Saint Mary's College in Raleigh, North Carolina (left), to the triumphant midnight mass Christmas procession in the grand Saint Louis cathedral in New Orleans (opposite).

◆

178

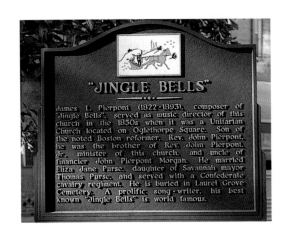

Directory

Almost every Southern town, from the smallest hamlet to bustling metropoli-

tan cities, opens its doors to visitors at Christmastime with special offerings

and celebrations. A quick call to any state's Department of Tourism or town's

Chamber of Commerce will provide locations, dates, and times of Christmas

events. But here are a few sources for you to check as you plan your own

Southern Christmas adventure. The homes, museums, and events listed and

marked by a ∾ are included in *Southern Christmas*.

SOUTHERN
CHRISTMAS
PLACES
∾

Alabama

Alabama Bureau of Tourism
532 South Perry Street
Montgomery, AL 36014-4614

∾ Bragg-Mitchell Mansion
906 Springhill Road
Mobile, AL 36607

Christmas in Historic Decatur
504 Walnut Street NE
Decatur, AL 35601

Constitution Hall Park
301 Madison Street
Huntsville, AL 35801

Fine Arts Museum of the South
P.O. Box 8425
Mobile, AL 36689

Arkansas

Arkansas Tourism Office
One Capitol Mall
Little Rock, AR 72201

Pioneer Village
P.O. Box 426
Rison, AK 71665

Delaware

Delaware Tourism Office
99 Kings Highway, Box 1401
Dover, DE 19903

Hagley Museum
P.O. Box 3630
Wilmington, DE 19807

∾ Yuletide Tours
Winterthur Museum
Winterthur, DE 19735

Florida

Florida Division of Tourism
125 West Van Buren Street
Tallahassee, FL 32301

∾ Historic St. Augustine
   Preservation Board
Government House
St. Augustine, FL 32084

∾ St. Augustine Historic Society
271 Charlotte Street
St. Augustine, FL 32084

∾ Walt Disney World-Christmas
P.O. Box 40
Lake Buena Vista, FL 32830

Winterfest
426 East Olas Blvd.
Ft. Lauderdale, FL 33301

Georgia

Callanwolde Fine Arts Center
980 Briarcliff Road, N.E.
Atlanta, GA 30306

∾Georgia Agirama
Box Q, Eighth St. at I-75
Tifton, GA 31794

Georgia Department of Industry
P.O. Box 1776
Atlanta, GA 30301

Jarrell Plantation
Rt. 1
Juliette, GA 31046

❧ Juliette Gordon Low Birthplace
Girl Scout National Center
142 Bull Street
Savannah, GA 31401

❧ New Echota Historic Site
Rt. 3
Calhoun, GA 30701

Westville's 1850 Christmas
P.O. Box 1850
Lumpkin, GA 31815

Kentucky

❧ Berea Welcome Center
201 North Broadway
Berea, KY 40403

Brennan House
631 South Fifth Street
Louisville, KY 40202

Headley-Whitney Museum
4435 Old Frankfort Pike
Lexington, KY 40510

Hunt-Morgan House
201 North Mill Street
Lexington, KY 40507

Kentucky Department of Travel
Development
Capitol Plaza Tower
Frankfort, KY 40601

Shakertown at Pleasant Hill
3500 Lexington Road
Harrodsburg, KY 40330

Louisiana

❧ A Creole Christmas
1008 N. Peters Street
New Orleans, LA 70116

Louisiana Office of Tourism
P.O. Box 94291
Baton Rouge, LA 70804-9291

Maryland

Hampton Mansion
535 Hampton Lane
Towson, MD 21204

Maryland Office of Tourism
Development
One Tourism Lane
Ridgely, MD 21660

Tourism Council of Annapolis
6 Dock Street
Annapolis, MD 21401

Mississippi

Mississippi Division of Tourism
P.O. Box 22825
Jackson, MS 39205

❧ Natchez Pilgrimage Tours
P.O. Box 347
Natchez, MS 39121

New Mexico

New Mexico Tourism & Travel
1100 St. Francis Drive
Santa Fe, NM 87503

❧ Santa Fe Chamber of
Commerce
P.O. Box 1928
Santa Fe, NM 87504

North Carolina

❧ Biltmore Estate
One North Pack Square
Asheville, NC 28801

Eastern Cabarrus Historical
Society, Inc.
Mt. Pleasant, NC 28124

❧ Greensboro Historical Museum
130 Summit Avenue
Greensboro, NC 27401

❧ The Grove Park Inn
290 Macon Avenue
Asheville, NC 28804

Hiddenite Center, Inc.
P.O. Box 311
Hiddenite, NC 28636

Liberty Hall
Box 634
Kenansville, NC 28349

Mordecai Historic Park
One Mimosa Drive
Raleigh, NC 27604

Museum of Early Southern
  Decorative Arts
P.O. Box 10310
Winston-Salem, NC 27108

North Carolina Division of Travel
430 N. Salisbury Street
Raleigh, NC 27603

Old Salem, Inc.
Drawer F, Salem Station
Winston-Salem, NC 27108

Schiele Museum
1500 Garrison Boulevard
Gastonia, NC 28502

Smith-McDowell Museum
283 Victoria Road
Asheville, NC 28801

Stagville Center
P.O. Box 71217
Durham, NC 27722-1217

Tryon Palace
P.O. Box 1007
New Bern, NC 28563

Oklahoma

Oklahoma Tourism and Recreation
500 Will Rogers Building
Oklahoma City, OK 73105

Territorial Christmas Celebration
P.O. Box 995
Guthrie, OK 73044

South Carolina

Christmas in Charleston
P.O. Box 975
Charleston, SC 29402

South Carolina Division of Tourism
P.O. Box 71
Columbia, SC 29202

Tennessee

The Hermitage
4580 Rachel's Lane
Hermitage, TN 37076-1331

Historic Jonesborough Visitors
  Center
P.O. Box 451
Jonesborough, TN 37659

Museum of Appalachia
P.O. Box 359
Norris, TN 378282

Opryland
2800 Opryland Drive
Nashville, TN 37219

Tennessee Department of Tourism
P.O. Box 23170
Nashville, TN 37202

Texas

Cowboys' Christmas Ball
P.O. Box 351
Anson, TX 79501

McFaddin-Ward House
1906 Mc Faddin Avenue
Beaumont, TX 77701

San Antonio Convention
  Bureau
P.O. Box 2277
San Antonio, TX 78298

Texas Tourism Division
P.O. Box 12008
Austin, TX 78711

Virginia

❧ Adam Thoroughgood House
1636 Parish Road
Virginia Beach, VA 23455

❧Colonial Williamsburg
Williamsburg, VA 32187

❧ Hunter House Museum
240 W. Freemason Street
Norfolk, VA 23510

❧ The Moses Myers House
323 East Freemason Street
Norfolk, VA 23510

Virginia Division of Tourism
1021 East Cary Street
Richmond, VA 23219

West Virginia

Travel West Virginia
State Capitol Complex
Charleston, WV 25305

SOUTHERN CHRISTMAS ITEMS

❧

When I find a lovely item or idea in a book that I would like to use in my home, one of my biggest problems is finding where to purchase materials. So many people have asked where I get some of the special items seen in these pages that I would like to share these addresses with you.

The Shop at the Historic
   New Orleans Collection
533 Royal Street
New Orleans, LA 70130
Spiral candles are hand-crafted by an order of monks

The Wizzard's Workbench
Rt. 13, Box 439, Indian Cave Road
Hendersonville, NC 28739.
Norma De Camp turns out one-of-a-kind family Santas

St. Claire Ices
140 Water Street
South Norwalk, CT 06854.
Wonderful Christmas motif ice creams are made by Bunny Brown, a North

Carolinian who moved north, and Barbara Zernike

Rebecca-Ruth Candy
P.O. Box 64
Frankfort, KY 40602.
For a true Southern Christmas treat, try their original Kentucky Bourbon Balls

Flag Fork Herb Farm
260 Flag Fork Road
Frankfort, KY 40601
Their catalog features grapevine trees and corn-shuck poinsettias, as well as other delightful folk art decorations

Laurel Springs Tree Farms
Box 85
Laurel Springs, NC 28644.
Beautiful, fresh tabletop Christmas trees like the one on the cover can be shipped to you

Acknowledgments

I will never forget the places I went, the people I met, or the stories I heard on my search to discover why Southern Christmases are so rich, so special. From our grand adventure I have wonderful tangible mementos—ornaments, photographs, little figures that will be lovingly added to our family's Christmas garden. And I have a store of experiences that I delight in sharing with others—the taste of mouth-watering Kentucky bourbon balls, the antebellum charm of Natchez, the dramatic beauty of the Appalachian mountains in wintertime. Then I have the memories which—unlike the trinkets and the shared experiences—cannot be displayed for others to see, nor talked about. I have laughable memories of silly times that are funny only to me, poignant memories of stories told to me from other people's hearts that now will live in my heart forever, and, of course, intimate, personal memories of the feeling that came with those twilight hours when the pink, blue, and azure tapestry of the Southern winter sky brought on lonesome times and I became travel-weary and homesick. But then a kind word or cheerful sight would change my mood and I'd say, "Come on Chip, we've got to get one more picture."

No matter what the hour or how busy everyone was, when I said "Southern Christmases," it was as if time stood still, work stopped, and Southern hospitality was lavished upon us. Thank each of you for sharing your time, objects, homes, resources, knowledge and reflections with me. And don't be surprised if you see me again. I can hardly wait for next Christmas!

Thank you Nancy Evans, Karol Schmiegel, Vi Riegel, and Jennifer Menson at Winterthur; Margaret Elinsky at the Hunter House Victorian Museum; Harriet Collins and Patrick Brennan at the Moses Myers House; Eric Turner, Cathlene Hinshaw and Ellen Rickman at the Biltmore Estate; Maggie Schlubach and Patricia Anne Miller at the Grove Park Inn; Bruce Johnson; Alison Hinsman at the Smith-McDowell Museum; Molly Thompson and Sue Henley in Jonesborough, Tennessee; John Rice Irwin at the Museum of Appalachia; Chuck Whiting at Opryland, USA; George Anderjack, Beth French, and Marsha Mullin at The Hermitage and Poplar Grove; Linda Evans at the Greensboro Historical Museum; Catherine Carstarphen and Chaplain Billy R. Miller at Stowe-Pharr Mills; Leona Buettner at the Ascension Lutheran Church; Kaye Anne Aikins; Ronald G. Wilson at Appomatox Court House National Historical Park; Mary Lynne Oglesby at The Callanwolde Fine Arts Center; Kay Williams, Susan Ferguson, and Maria LaFargue at Tryon Palace; Tom Kenan, Rich Boyd, and Dot Rawlings at Liberty Hall; Cookie O'Brien and Michael Wells at the De Mesa-Sanchez House; Eddie Joyce Geyer at "The Oldest House"; Richard F. Carlson and Timothy C. Hargus at the Ballastone Inn; Marilyn and John Whelpley; Norma DeCamp; Stephen Bohlin-Davis, Katherine Keena, and Fran Powell at the Juliette Gordon Low Birthplace; Amy B. Blyth at the Charleston Trident Convention & Visitors Bureau, the members of the

College of Charleston Counseling Center who allowed us to join their progressive Southern Christmas dinner at the John Rutledge House Inn, Two Unity Alley, and Elliott House Inn; Bonnie Leigh Brake at the John Rutledge House Inn; Sue Avenel, Lydia Hopson, Sam Kirby, Carolyn Lee, B.J. Sanders, and Tracey Tood at the Edmondston-Alston House; Mary Hart, Sarah Lytle, Kris Kepford-Young, and Donna Owens at Middleton Place; Pat Phillips, John H. Johnson, and Christine Tibbetts at the Georgia Agrirama; Nancy Holmes; Patrice Baur at the Bragg-Mitchell House; Ernest A. Loeffler, Jr. of the San Antonio Convention & Visitors Bureau; Jessica Foye, Gary Smith, Glenda Dyer, Mathew White, Judith Walker Linsley, Richard Howard, Jackie Jones and Kenny Sanderfer at the McFaddin-Ward House; Judy Stone at the Beaumont Convention & Visitors Bureau; Robert DeBlieux of the Natchez Pilgrimage Tours; Ron Miller at the Historic Natchez Foundation; William F. Heins, II and Nancy Gibbs at Dunleith; Louise Burns at Longwood; Virginia and Lowell Langdon Morrison of Green Leaves; Peter Kovacs, Joe Samrow, Jr., and Matt Scallin; Alma H. Neal at the Beauregard-Keyes House; Cathy Clements, Douglas Leman, and Jeffry Landesberg at The Pontchartrain Hotel; Charlotte Hoggatt at The Historic New Orleans Collection;

Ann Masson and Harriet Bos at Gallier House; Tamra Carboni at the 1850 House; Charles Mackie at the Hermann-Grima Historic House; Macon Riddle of Let's Go Antiquing; the staff at St. Louis Cathedral; Sarah Williamson, Sis Cheshire, Ginny Stevens, and Sally Poland of the Mordecai Square Historic Society; Betty Tyson and Martha Battle at the North Carolina Division of Archives and History; Martha Stoops, Marti Smith, Christine Thomson, Sarah Johnson, Mary Pearson, Gloria Graham, Faye Fussell, and the Alumni Decorating Committee at Saint Mary's College; Delores Sanders of Home Moravian Church, Winston-Salem; Paula Lochlair, Linda Therrell, Tonya Smith and Gene Capps at Old Salem; Sally Gant at the Museum of Early Southern Decorative Arts; Ed Berry of The Shop in Sante Fe; Sara Evans of Creative Images Limited; Jeff Stancil at New Echota Historic Site; Nettie Lee of the Anson Chamber of Commerce; and Jennifer F. Goldsborough at the Maryland Historical Society, Sam Hill at the University of Florida; Tom Parramore; Lovey Midget of Rodanthe; Deborah Lessner and Lisa Pitman of Wilmington, North Carolina; Hugh Morton; Wade Yarborough; Frank Stoner and Bob Timberlake; Rebekah Vohosca at Walt Disney World; Ken Wolf, Libby Oliver, Patrick Saylor, and Susan Berg at Colonial Williamsburg; Sandra O'Keefe at

Lloyd House; Nora Shepard and Katherine Bratton; Debbie Padgett; Mary Staney; Garry Barker and Ed Ford at Berea College; Stephanie Carcano and Marilyn Sinkey at the Adam Thoroughgood House; William Woys Weaver; Mary Williams; Betty Dernam Hunt; Rachel Pabst; Carol Herner and Stephen Boyd; Joan Battle; Art and Helen White; Marion Gregory; Pat and Lewis Gaskin; Frances King; Lynn McCarthy; and Larry Sherwood and Ann Cahn who believed in this project from the first.

At home I can never sufficiently thank Carlton Long for his help, advice, and cheerfulness—year round—or Jean Ann Anderson who kept Saint Mary's Christmas functions running so smoothly no one knew I wasn't there. Thank you, Marie Wright, Betsy Burnish and Lisa Vaughan for manning our offices so smoothly.

Special heart-felt thanks go to my friends at Crown—Ken Sansone, Sharon Squibb, Etya Pinker, Linda Gelbard, Gail Shanks, Barbara Marks, Chesie Hortenstine, Pam Shepard, Betty Prashker, Michelle Sidrane and Chip Gibson—who know Southern Christmases should be shared.

My love this and every Christmas to Clauston, Joslin and Langdon, Mother and Daddy, all the Jenkins, Joslins, Brockwells, and Matthews, the Henderson clan, Janella, Mary Jane and Doug, Buck and Lucy, John and Ann, Elizabeth Reid Murray, and Hazel Buchanan.

Credits

PHOTO CREDITS

In addition to the credits given in the text, these credits are gratefully acknowledged: Adam Thoroughgood House, Norfolk, VA, p. 15, 111; Atlantic Insurance Company of Savannah, GA, p. 74; Ballastone Inn, Savannah, GA, pp. 3, 184; Colonial Williamsburg, Williamsburg, VA, pp. 3, 6, 7, 14, 32, 51, 52, 102, 158, 171; De Mesa-Sanchez House, St. Augustine, FL, pp. 15, 27; Edmondston-Alston House, Charleston, SC, pp. 26, 27, 128; Flagler Hospital, St. Augustine, FL. p. 184; Georgia Agrirama, Tifton, GA, pp. 103, 125, 176; Green Leaves, Natchez, MS, pp. 83, 153, 186; Grove Park Inn, Asheville, NC, p. 75; Hall House, Salisbury, NC, p. 86; Herman-Grimma House, New Orleans, LA, pp. 57, 122; Henry Frances duPont Winterthur Museum, DE, pp. 86, 122; Hunter House Museum, Norfolk, VA, pp. 7, 68; Juliette Gordon Low Birthplace, Savannah, GA, p. 111; John Rutledge House Inn, Charleston, SC, p. 21; Kentucky Treasure Chest, Frankfort, KY, p. 62; Liberty Hall, Kenansville, NC, pp. 101, 125; Lloyd House Library, Alexandria, VA, p. 56; Log House Sales Room, Berea, KY, p. 17; Longwood, Natchez, MS, p. 150; McFaddin-Ward House, Beaumont, TX, p. 128; Middleton Place, Charleston, SC, p. 128; Mordecai House, Raleigh, NC, pp. 93, 132; Moses Myers House, Norfolk, VA, pp. 123, 135; Museum of Appalachia, Norris, TN, pp. 137, 148; Naff-Baxter-Henley House, Jonesborough, TN, pp. 83, 176; New Orleans City Park, p. 161; Old Salem, Winston-Salem, NC, pp. 6, 137, 159; The Oldest House, St. Augustine Historical Society, FL, p. 173; Opryland Hotel, Nashville, TN, pp. 159, 161, 186; Roughwood Collection courtesy of William Woys Weaver, pp. 108, 130; San Antonio, TX, photographs by Al Rendon, courtesy of the San Antonio Convention & Visitors Bureau, p. 169; Saint Mary's College, Raleigh, NC, pp. 15, 173, 176; Santa Fe, NM, photographs by R. R. Twarog, p. 109; Stone Mountain, GA, p. 157; Timberlake Originals, pp. 8, 137, 187; Tryon Palace, New Bern, NC, p. 51; Valentine Museum, Richmond, VA, p. 151; Marilyn and John Whelpley, Savannah, GA, pp. 54, 82.

TEXT CREDITS

"Why Southern Christmases": p. 17 (and mentioned throughout the book), Thomas Nelson Page. *The Old South*. New York: Scribner, 1982; pp. 19–20, Stanley Kimmel. *Mr. Davis's Richmond*. New York: Coward-McCann, 1958; pp. 22, Hope Summerell Chamberlain. *Old Days in Chapel Hill, Being the Life and Letters of Cornelia Phillips Spencer*. Chapel Hill: University of North Carolina Press, 1926; p. 22, Hunter Dickinson Farish, editor. *Journal & Letters of Philip Vickers Fithian, 1773–1774: A Plantation Tutor of the Old Dominion*. Charlottesville: University Press of Virginia, 1943.

"Christmas Trees": p. 64, Katherine Batts Salley, editor. *Life at Saint Mary's*. Chapel Hill: University of North Carolina Press, 1942.

"Santa and Christmas Gifts": p. 91, Julia Peterkin. *A Plantation Christmas*. Boston: Houghton Mifflin Company, 1942; pp. 93 and 94, Roark Bradford. *How Come Christmas*. New York: Harper & Brothers, 1930; p. 94, James Mellon, editor. *Bullwhip Days: The Slaves Remember*. New York: Grove Weidenfeld, 1988; p. 94, Susan Dabney Smedes. *A Southern Planter*. New York: James Pott, 1890; p. 95, Kemp Plummer Battle. *Memories of an Old-Time Tarheel*. Edited by William James Battle. Chapel Hill: University of North Carolina Press, 1945; p. 95, Beth Crabtree and James W. Patton, editors. *Journal of a Secesh Lady: The Diary of Catherine Ann Devereux Edmonston, 1860*. Raleigh: North Carolina Department of Cultural Resources, Historical Publication Section, 1979; p. 99, *The Little Colonel's Christmas Vacation*. New York: L.C. Page, 1905; p. 100, Frances Parkinson Keyes. *A Christmas Gift*. New York: Hawthorne Books, 1959.

"Fireworks & Mummers": p. 107, Mrs. A. J. Ellis. "Christmas in Dixie During the War Between the States." Raleigh: North Carolina Department of Cultural Resources, Division of Archives and History, circa 1930.

"Christmas Dinners, Parties, and Weddings": pp. 127–128, Private papers of Juliette Gordon Low. Birthplace, Savannah, Georgia; p. 129, Mrs. A. J. Ellis. "Christmas in Dixie During the War Between the States." Raleigh: North Carolina Department of Cultural Resources, Division of Archives and History, circa 1930; p. 130, Julia Peterkin. *A Plantation Christmas*. Boston: Houghton Mifflin Company, 1942.

"Country Christmases": p. 139, Ellen Mordecai. "Gleanings from Long Ago." Raleigh: Capital Area Preservation, Inc. 1933; p. 147, "The Adoration." From *Bow Down in Jericho*. New York: Dutton, 1950; p. 148, Lillian Smith. *Memory of a Large Christmas*. New York: W. W. Norton, 1962.

"Civil War Christmases": p. 152, Beth Crabtree and James W. Patton, editors. *Journal of a Secesh Lady: The Diary of Catherine Ann Devereux Edmonston, 1860*. Raleigh: North Carolina Department of Cultural Resources, Historical Publication Section, 1979; pp. 153 and 154, Ina May Ogletree McAdams. *The Building of "Longwood."* Austin: self-published, 1972; p. 154, Mrs. A. J. Ellis. "Christmas in Dixie During the War Between the States." Raleigh: North Carolina Department of Cultural Resources, Division of Archives and History, circa 1930.

"Christmases Old & New": p. 159, Phyllis McGinley. "City Christmas." From *Merry Christmas, Happy New Year*. New York: Curtis Brown Ltd., 1958.

Index